D1397429

THE
NOISE
IN THE SKY

THE
NOISE
IN THE SKY

Minton C. Johnston

ABINGDON PRESS
Nashville and New York

THE NOISE IN THE SKY

Copyright © 1968 by Abingdon Press

Library of Congress Catalog Card Number: 68-25361

SET UP, PRINTED, AND BOUND BY THE
PARTHENON PRESS, AT NASHVILLE,
TENNESSEE, UNITED STATES OF AMERICA

PREFACE
and
DEDICATION

It is difficult to choose titles. They should be arresting, but they should also be expressive to some degree of what is inside the covers. The problem was settled for me by an eight-year-old boy, as you can read in the first chapter. He called the revelation which came to his fairy prince and princess a "noise in the sky." I can hardly do better than follow his example.

Lest the reference seem too childish, let us remember that on two occasions a noise in the sky came to bring comfort, encouragement, and faith to Jesus of Nazareth, first at his baptism and a second time when he was entering Jerusalem. Some people explained it away by saying that it thundered; others that an angel spoke to him; but for Jesus it was clearly the voice of his Father.

The voice in the sky may not come to us, but the voice of God has, both in the Bible and through the Holy Spirit to our souls. This book simply tries to express in many different ways what it seems to me that voice is saying. Of course John put it more concisely, simply, and clearly when he wrote,

"God is light" and "God is love." If all that follows helps us to realize the truth of those simple statements, this book will have done its work.

I dedicate this book to all the childlike in heart who Jesus said would inherit the Kingdom and, particularly, to Mark Allen, whose school composition started it off.

CONTENTS

THE NOISE IN THE SKY

A proud father handed me a composition his eight-year-old boy had written. It was called "The Fairy Prince and Princess." Here is the story.

"Once upon a time there lived a Prince and a Princess. They would go out into the woods by themselves. One time when they were out they heard this funny noise. It scared them. They were frightened. They started to run, but it was coming the way they were going. They started to cry and cry. The Prince said, 'Crying will do no good. We must stop crying and be brave until someone comes to get us.' So they were brave. Just then they heard this noise in the sky. It said, 'Do not be afraid.'"

The teacher wrote at the top, "Very good, but no ending." It was that comment which disturbed the father. Had it really no ending?

Maybe if Mark had written, "and they all lived happily ever after," the teacher would have been satisfied. But did they? Does anyone? Romantic novels end with wedding bells, but if you have been married, you know that that isn't the end. No story has an ending really. All it does is conclude one particular chapter of life, but life itself goes on and on.

The Acts of the Apostles is like that. Luke didn't end it; he just stopped writing. He took Paul to

Rome, lodged him in a prison, and left him there. What happened afterward? Scholars have been asking that question ever since. Why did Luke stop there? Perhaps he wanted to suggest that there *is* no final ending—that the story is still going on, past Paul, past the persecutions, the dark ages, the Reformation, on to today and past today.

What we need is not an ending but something that makes an ending impossible, some discovery which carries the story on to infinity. That is what Luke did in the Acts. I think that is what Mark Allen had in mind in the story he wrote.

When Mark's father was telling me about the story, he got the last part twisted. He thought the last words were "They heard this noise in the sky. It said, 'Do not be afraid.' So they were brave." Probably most of us would have written it that way, but not Mark. He had them being brave first, and then they heard the noise in the sky which said, "Do not be afraid." Mark wrote that the prince called for courage, and they were brave. *Then* they heard the noise which had terrified them, saying "Do not be afraid." Courage comes first, Mark implied, then the revelation.

"Out of the mouths of babes and sucklings!" Eight-year-old Mark has something to say to all of us. How many there are who are waiting for something to make us brave, something to happen to change our lives. We are waiting for that noise in the sky to bring a message of encouragement, meanwhile cowering before it in terror. But it doesn't happen that way. Mark is right. The prince must first say, "We must be brave," and then *be* brave, before the other happens.

That is one of the best illustrations of faith that I've come across. Perhaps we'll believe it if an eight-year-old boy writes it when we miss it in the eleventh chapter of Hebrews. The fairy prince and princess are blood kin to Noah, Abraham, Moses, and all the other heroes in that grand chapter.

Faith is acting on a conviction, dim perhaps, but inescapable—going ahead in the darkness and finding the proof afterwards. Faith is not the blinding sunlight of noon but a gleam in the darkness. Faith is the belief that crying will do no good, that it is incumbent on a prince to be brave, and then *be* brave—not because conditions have changed, but because being brave is the only way to be.

Then does the dreadful noise in the sky turn into a message of hope and encouragement? Yes, I'm sure it does, but perhaps not always as quickly as Mark suggested. Faith is not always rewarded instantly, sometimes not even before we die. Remember that in Hebrews 11 there is a list of unnamed heroes of whom is written, "These all . . . received not the promise: God having provided some better thing for us, that they without us should not be made perfect."

That chapter in Hebrews is but a small section of the unfinished story in which each of us has a part to play in courage and faith.

11

SHUT DOORS AND FORBIDDEN JOYS

One evening I opened the door to the back bed-room. From somewhere the cat heard the door open, and she dashed in and scooted under the low bed beyond my reach. When she wouldn't come out, I went away, leaving the door open. In her own sweet time she came out by herself. Another room that was once a summer kitchen we keep closed also because both rooms are un-heated. The cat is firmly persuaded that we are hiding something wonderful in those rooms. Shut doors are an irresistible attraction to her.

Though they say curiosity killed the cat, we humans have enough of it ourselves. Shut doors are as much a challenge to us as to the cat. For instance, there is the Greek myth about Pan-dora's box. Pandora was the Greek Eve, the first created woman, who was given a closed box by the gods and warned on no account ever to open it. But curiosity got the better of her. She opened the box the merest fraction to peek inside, and all the evils known to man leaped out and scattered over the earth. Only one thing remained in the box—hope.

The third chapter of Genesis is strikingly similar to this Greek myth. There also we have the for-bidden something, the curiosity which overcame

Adam and Eve, and the curse which fell on them and all their descendants. Apparently the most challenging and intriguing words in the world seemed to be "Thou shalt not!"

They still *are* to the natural man. Unfortunately too many Christians have the same viewpoint. They look on God as the one who is always saying, "Thou shalt not!" They suspect that the things which are forbidden would be very enjoyable if only they had nerve enough to try them. So religion for them consists in the number of things they don't do, reluctantly. They believe that if they deprive themselves on earth, they'll make up for it in heaven. That is what upsets so many people when an out-and-out sinner repents on his death-bed and is converted. They wonder, is that wretch going to get into heaven just the same as we who have been good all our lives and didn't do many things we wanted to do? The repentant sinner on his deathbed seems to many people the supreme example of eating one's cake and having it too. How many of us would like to try it if only we could be sure we'd be able to repent in time!

Well, is Christianity simply doing without things on earth so we can have them in heaven? Or is it, both on earth and in heaven, having doors open to a much more wonderful, exciting, and joyful life?

While the law proclaimed, "Thou shalt not!" Christ came proclaiming, "Thou shalt!" The law, said Paul, was a schoolmaster to bring us to Christ. Children have to be told not to do things, but mature people should be able to see *why* those things are forbidden and, by their own common sense and through the example of others, discover where the real and lasting joys are.

That is what Christ came to tell and show. That is what the disciples saw in him and what the world saw in the disciples and in the early Christians. It was something wonderfully attractive, and the world wanted it. People should see the same thing in us today, for there is no way in which they can be wooed away from the spurious and harmful attractions of the shut doors except by showing to them the real treasures of the doors which Christ opened.

Again and again my mind turns to what Paul said was the fruit of the Spirit, "love, joy, peace, longsuffering, gentleness, goodness, faith, meekness, temperance." The first three particularly are things every human being longs for. These are things which every Christian should have and show, for they are the gift of God. If we really did have them and showed them unmistakably to the world, then the world wouldn't be clamoring so much for the shut doors and the forbidden fruit.

Nor would we.

A PAIN IN THE NECK?

I started to read *Burma Surgeon* again and found it difficult to keep at it. It is too excitingly interesting. Every page or so Dr. Gordon Seagrave had something to say which made me want to discuss it with him—or with you or with anyone. It is one of the most vivid books I've come across and Dr. Seagrave one of the most vivid, likable, and Christian men one could ever hope to meet.

All the same he must have been a thorn in the flesh to many regular missionaries. He expressed it more colloquially. "As a missionary," he wrote, "I was a most unorthodox pain in the neck." Apparently there were two reasons. For one thing, he put the healing of bodies first. It was his job, not just a means to get in some preaching—like the magic tricks of a medicine man. He wanted a first-class hospital with first-class nurses, giving first-class treatment. And he got it. Now that might not please some of the people at home who give their hard-earned money to convert the heathen (about two dollars a year for every Christian in America!). No, it probably offended many orthodox Christians, but I am sure that it pleased Dr. Seagrave's Master, who went about doing good and to whose healing ministry so much of the Gospel account is devoted.

Then too Dr. Seagrave had a most unorthodox sense of humor as the words "pain in the neck" suggest. He tells how, being on leave, he preached in a large American church. The minister so liked the sermon that he took Dr. Seagrave for a ride in his large new Cadillac. On the way he asked, "Is it true that you are not only a missionary but also the son of a missionary?" Dr. Seagrave admitted the impeachment and added that a grandfather and two great-grandfathers had been missionaries too. The minister exclaimed in wonder, "Then how does it happen that you are not an imbecile?"

I like Dr. Seagrave's humor in quoting that conversation, and I liked it especially because I knew the minister, the Cadillac and the attitude. Inwardly I cheered for Seagrave.

Both Dr. Seagrave's work and his humor might seem to some people to be a deterrent to missions, but for me they go together and make for real Christianity and for the real work of missions. The first is concern for people, for sick bodies, bewildered minds and sinful natures—but above all, concern. Seagrave cared and cared desperately. If his first concern was for bodies, those of us sitting at home hardly dare to criticize. After all, our two-dollars-a-year average hardly permits that.

The second thing, humor, is for me one of the main requirements for and one of the finest fruits of religion. After all, Paul said the fruit of the Spirit was love, joy, and peace, and surely humor is part of that. I dare to say that no one has a true religion until he has learned to laugh. Humor is a sense of proportion. It is taking God so seriously that one doesn't need to take himself or anyone or anything else too seriously. It is seeing life as filled with God. It is walking through the fields and by the seaside with Jesus. It is understanding not only his concern for the bodies and souls of men, but sharing his patience, feeling his love, and appre-

16

ciating his humor. For like Dr. Seagrave's book, the Gospels are filled with the humor of Jesus.

It may seem strange to combine a tremendous concern with sparkling humor. A surgeon sees all the sorrows, the sicknesses, and the misery of men. Seagrave saw more, for he was not only a missionary doctor but went through the war in Burma as well. He saw griefs and tragedies at first hand, but beyond them he saw the glory of God and the companionship of Jesus Christ. He doesn't say so, but he reveals it page after page.

Yes, he may have called himself a pain in the neck to other missionaries, but I'm sure he was a joy to Jesus Christ, his Master.

"I WANT MY DADDY!"

One Sunday the long prayer was interrupted. It had just nicely started, the congregation was sitting with bowed heads and closed eyes, everything was quiet, when suddenly there came a loud voice from the back stairs next to the pulpit. It was a complaining, emphatic, tearful voice. The door burst open, and the intruder came running in, stopped directly in front of the pulpit, and shouted, "I want my Daddy!"

A four-year-old boy, just promoted from the nursery to the kindergarten, apparently took a dim view of the change. He was lonely, disconsolate, and afraid. He wanted his daddy. He knew where his daddy was, so he came and hollered. He knew what he wanted and said so—there was no mistaking that!

The congregation remained bowed, but most of them had one eye open and all were smiling. I told the youngster to go to the back where his daddy was and waited until he had trotted down the aisle and found him. Then the prayer was continued.

Or had it ever stopped? That is the question.

Fortunately our church takes incidents of that kind in its stride. I think God takes them in his stride too. Or perhaps I should say that for God it wasn't an interruption at all but the main business of the day. Were my words in front of the congregation or their thoughts or the ordered dignity of the service as important to God as one small boy who needed his daddy? No, I think the boy came first, and I think the story in the Gospels about Jesus and the children whom the disciples would have driven away proves it. "Let the children come to me," Jesus said, "don't stop them." So after all it was God's main business.

After the interruption, though, the prayer didn't go on as it had started. A new train of thought had been introduced which could not be ignored. Was there anything more important that we could say to God than a small boy had said when he cried, "I want my Daddy"?

Is that too familiar a term to apply to Almighty

God? Shouldn't it be something high-sounding and sonorous like Lord God Jehovah? While we should certainly reverence God, reverence wasn't what he asked for first—but love. And love doesn't insist on high-sounding titles. Love delights in affectionate terms. The small boy didn't want his "father," he wanted his "daddy." Underneath that is what we all want, someone who loves us and whom we love, someone who will hold us tight in his arms, smooth our hair and wipe the tears away, smile into our eyes and make us know we are safe with him.

Without Jesus that approach to God would be impossible, but Jesus has shown us that that is exactly the kind of thing God wants. The appeal of Jesus is not to the very righteous or the self-sufficient, but to the sinful, scared, lonely, love-starved, and hopeless. He makes them believe that God wants to put his arms around them, comfort them, and make them know that he loves them and will never let them go.

Augustine in his *Confessions* put the idea in loftier words: "Thou hast made us for thyself, and our hearts are restless until they find their rest in thee." That just says what the little boy said, "I want my daddy." His cry is our cry too. Whether we know it or not, confess it or not, it is our cry too.

However, we mustn't stop there. It is not enough to recognize the little boy's cry as the basic cry of our own souls; we must know it as the cry of the world. Often that isn't easy. There are so many other voices, so many other cries. There are so many people, old and young, feverishly seeking all manner of things, that the cry is drowned out and the unobservant and unsympathetic may miss it entirely.

But God hasn't missed it. God knows what is wrong with his world and with us. He knows that, despite all our other cries, we have only one fundamental desire, to find him, to find our daddy, our Father in heaven. That is why Jesus came, that is what Jesus did, that is the meaning of the Gospels. God is answering a cry which he alone can hear, the cry of the soul for him. Read again the fifteenth chapter of Luke about the boy who thought he wanted so many other things but finally found he wanted just one, his daddy.

That is what we all want. And there is God, like the small boy's daddy, waiting to hear us cry out and come to take us into his arms.

LONG WORDS AND GOOD NEWS

When people want to appear very learned, they use long words, sesquipedalian words. Now, that's a good example—sesquipedalian. Its meaning is really quite simple—very long words.

I object to long words on principle, but most of all in religion. They are confusing, and the harm they have done to religion is beyond computing. I'm thinking especially of some particular words, *evangelism, evangelistic, evangelical,* and a good old Anglo-Saxon word which has gone out of general usage except in religion, *gospel.* Personally I wouldn't mind throwing them all away and using instead the plain and simple English words they really mean—good news. The evangel is good news, evangelism is telling it, an evangelist one who tells it, and the gospel is "God's spiel," God's word, which is good news too.

All this came to my mind when I read a church notice which advertised that that particular church preached the gospel, with the emphasis on the word *the.* The implication was that it was the only church, or one of the very few, which did. So when I read the words "the gospel," I started off to try and find for myself what the gospel really was.

Well, I see I've fallen into the trap myself. What I wanted to discover was the good news. I came across it first right at the beginning of Christ's ministry. Mark, in the fourteenth verse of the first chapter, wrote that Christ came "preaching the gospel of the kingdom of God." So the kingdom of God was the great good news that Jesus said he had come to bring. Perhaps that doesn't sound very much like what some declare *the* gospel is, but there it is in black and white.

Then I read further, and in II Corinthians 4:4 in the King James Version I came across the words "the glorious gospel of Christ." Idly I looked at the verse in the Greek, looked again, and took up the phone and called a scholar friend. He and I discussed it together and I later found confirmation of our conclusions in the New English Bible, one of the latest scholarly translations. There the phrase read, "the gospel of the glory of Christ," just as my friend and I thought it should. In I Timothy too where the King James Version reads "according to the glorious gospel of the blessed God," the New English Bible reads "the gospel which tells of the glory of God in his eternal felicity."

Well, let's put that in simple English too. It is the good news of the glory of Christ and the good news of how wonderful God is.

How do you react to that? I was thrilled! The evangel, or evangelistic, or evangelical, or gospel, or, right down to where we live, the good news, is about God himself, how wonderful Christ is, how loving, forgiving, friendly, patient, sacrificing—yes, how altogether glorious Christ is.

You see, the good news isn't about you or me. It is about him—then about us. It isn't first of all about our getting into heaven and how we can get there, but about heaven itself. As the hymn "The Sands of Time Are Sinking" says,

> The Lamb is all the glory
> Of Emmanuel's land.

That is the good news my soul really wants to hear, good news I can understand and welcome. If the good news is about the glory of Christ, if it is about his kingdom—that he is really on the throne

—if it is about God himself, then I don't need to worry any longer about my stupidity in failing to understand long words or intricate doctrines. I don't need to fret about trying to find some complicated, twisted, hidden road to heaven and being forever afraid I'll miss it. The good news isn't the road; it is Christ the Good Shepherd who went off into the wilderness to find one lost lamb. I'm that lamb, and all I need to know is that this wonderful Christ loves me and has come to save me. To me that is the real good news—*the* gospel.

RUNNING WATER AND CONTENTMENT

We now have running water at the cottage. I think we earned it. For twenty summers we (I, mostly) carried all our water from the lake in pails. And we had what might be termed outside "inconveniences." In wet or cold weather that was what they were.

Now we are modern and civilized, but I'm not sure that we really are so much better off. Yes, it is more convenient, comfortable, and up-to-date, but that isn't what *makes* a cottage. The view across the lake to the islands, the golden path of the sun as it nears setting, the crimson glory of the sunset, the whisper of the breeze in the evergreens—these are worth all the trappings of civilization if one had to choose. The conveniences are pleasant extras.

I am reminded that Paul told the Philippians that he had learned in whatsoever state he was therewith to be content. As he was writing from a Roman prison, that is some statement. Of course he liked to be rich (he called it "to abound")— everyone does—but he also knew how to be poor (to be abased). The trappings of civilization meant little to him because there was something else which meant so much more. He accepted those trappings gratefully when they were offered and did without them cheerfully when they were denied. But there was that one thing he could not do without, which made poverty or riches a secondary matter; that was the presence of Christ and the privilege of serving him.

This brings up two important questions. The first is to put *things,* especially the luxuries of life, in their rightful place. I asked a newcomer from England what real differences he found in Canada. His answer surprised me. He said that in Canada no one ever admitted that they couldn't afford something. I wonder if that is true? Probably it is, to a rather terrifying extent, for if it *is* true, it is terrifying. It means we have put *things* first, things like running water, expensive motorboats, the latest model cars, automatic washers, and all the rest. Now I have no fault to find with any of these—after all, we do now have running water at the cottage. My complaint is that *things* have usurped the place of something far more important.

Perhaps this almost universal attitude is partly

responsible for the shortage of men in the ministry. But let's not be too hard on either the ministers or those who were called but turned aside. They are simply tainted with the common complaint, the desire for things. We all want above all else to abound and are content only when we do. But are we really content even then?

At the cottage it isn't, as I said, running water but the lake, the trees, the sunset, the view across the water. In life it isn't things, surely, but the presence of and fellowship with Jesus Christ. And because we cannot remain in that fellowship or continue to enjoy that presence without it, it is serving Christ.

Perhaps the term "serving Christ" is too vague. It simply means doing the tasks he has given us to do, realizing that they are from him, for him, and to promote his kingdom.

With Paul it meant enduring a Roman prison. With us it could mean doing our work in factory, home, store, school, or wherever we are placed, in a trustworthy, honest, cheerful, and Christian manner.

When that goal takes hold of our hearts and becomes the one important fact in our lives, then the means to accomplish it will come with it. If it is best done in poverty, then that's what we'll have; if in wealth, that we'll have too. But in poverty or wealth, the trappings of life will be for one purpose, to help us to minister to him who loved us and gave himself for us.

ONE PLACE OR MANY?

A wife was being driven nearly frantic by her husband's violin playing. He was a good player, but hour after hour and day after day he played, and he played only one note. Finally she burst out, "Why do you play only one note? Elman plays other notes, Kreisler plays other notes. Why do you play only one note?"

Her husband sniffed and said, "They are looking for the place. I've found it."

Of course he was crazy. But maybe there are others like him. So many claim to have found the place, the one note. They are certain of it.

Well, how certain can we be in religious matters that we have truly found that one note? Unfortunately so many claims conflict. It must be confusing for ordinary people who listen to all the claims to decide among all the notes which one is right.

Probably none are. Yet perhaps all are. Probably each has found one aspect of the truth, for after all the violinist who played just one note did have that note right. But just as certainly no single mortal has all the truth, nor even the *whole* truth of that one thing he has found. That is our problem, but it is also one of the grand things about religion. We are in pursuit of something too great for mortal man to know completely, yet something of which we can find hints and clues and revelations opening up all around us.

One of the most dogmatic men in the Bible was Paul. He laid down the law, and most properly so, as any person who has found truth must do. But Paul wasn't as cocksure as we sometimes imagine. He said in one of his best-known passages, "now we see through a glass, darkly, . . . now I know in part." He saw as though he were looking through a clouded glass. He could see something surely, but the details were vague.

I remember once having to borrow a pair of spectacles at an old folks' home where I was to hold a service. I had left mine at home so an old gentleman kindly lent me his. I could just make out the words of the scripture and hymns, but the edges were blurred and fuzzy, and I got some of the words wrong. Paul might have said that we look through spectacles made for eyes other than ours. Human beings looking through God's glasses naturally find them difficult to see through clearly.

However, Paul declared that he did see, even though he did not see perfectly. And we also should make that claim, both that we do see and that we don't see perfectly. We see in part, we know in part, but to a certain extent we *do* see and we *do* know.

No, we haven't found the one note, not completely. There is no revelation or aspect of God, no doctrine of men or truth of religion which we have plumbed to its depth or of which we have reached the topmost height. No human being has ever done that, or ever can until at last we see God face to face. But every one of us—I say every one advisedly—every one of us has discovered something. We may not see it perfectly, but we have seen it. Yes, we've seen it even though we may not like it and are perversely unwilling to follow it.

It is the discovery of that one thing, that one part of the total truth, which should be the place we begin. We must not harp on that one note exclusively nor claim complete certainty, but from it we should go on to discover others. Every tune begins with one note. All music is one note following another. And the greatest music of all is the symphony in which many instruments playing many notes make perfect harmony. All truth is first one part of truth, discovered, followed, and added to.

Then, as Paul declared, some day we shall know. We shall see, not through a glass darkly, but face to face. And the beauty of the truth we have now found will then be paled into insignificance by the glory of the whole truth which shall then be revealed to us.

WHERE THE DEVIL OBJECTS

Some years ago I was invited to preach in a church which was holding some special celebration. Because it was a special evening there were a good many musical numbers, and it was fairly late when it came time for the sermon. Everything had gone quietly enough to that point, but no sooner had I stood up to preach than an interruption occurred. A bat appeared from some remote recess and swooped back and forth, back and forth. During the whole twenty minutes of the sermon it swooped and darted. I found it a bit disturbing. It didn't help me preach or others listen and rather hindered my sermon about the lordship of Christ.

No sooner had the sermon ended, however, than the bat disappeared. Then we went downstairs to a so-called fireside hour (with no fireside, of course). There we had more musical numbers, and after they were over, a bit to my surprise, I was again asked to speak. I got up rather hesitantly for I thought I'd said all I needed to say. Without any hesitation whatever the bat appeared in the basement and again swooped round my head. A deacon got a broom. After three vicious swipes he connected, and the bat fell to the floor within an inch of my heel.

I looked down at it, surely the most repellent in

looks of any animal. As it lay there it reminded me of the traditional pictures of the devil. And it reminded me also of a verse from Genesis: "It shall bruise thy head, and thou shalt bruise his heel."

I hadn't appreciated the bat's interference with the sermon, and I guess the bat repented of it too, seeing what finally happened to it, but suddenly I thought it might be for the best after all. Though few people ever remember a sermon, I doubt if any present that evening ever forgot that bat. Maybe they also remembered what I said after the bat was finally disposed of.

I told them that to me the bat resembled the devil, reminded them that I had been preaching about the lordship of Christ, and that only while I was preaching upstairs and stood up to speak downstairs had the bat appeared. Then I stated my conviction that the devil does not object to any preaching or any doctrine of Christianity save one—the lordship of Christ. He doesn't mind anyone believing in God or believing anything he likes about Christ or having any Christian faith whatsoever, provided he doesn't give allegiance and obedience to Jesus.

And of course there is the tradition that the devil was once the leading archangel in heaven but became the devil because he rebelled against God.

Now I am not asking you to believe in the devil—you may please yourself about that—but somehow we have to take into account the power of evil existing in the world wherever it comes from. Whatever we do believe about it, surely the old tradition and our own common sense join together to enforce one fact—that the only saving faith is obedience to God and the only thing which finally condemns us is our refusal to obey him.

When the Christian church came into being there was then, as there is now, much that the Christians didn't know and very much more that they didn't understand. But there was one thing that the youngest, the most ignorant, and the most stupid did know, one thing which everyone had to follow if he claimed to be a Christian at all. So at baptism each was required to say two words, *"Christos Kurios"*—Jesus Christ is Lord.

I believe that is all that God requires today. Not even the wisest among us fully understands God, and God himself knows all too well that most of us are puzzled and bewildered about many doctrines. But one thing each of us does know, can understand and can do, and is required to do . . . make Jesus Christ our Lord and follow him.

WITH ALL MY WORLDLY GOODS

I was listening to a devotional address and I got very restless. The speaker told us we had to make Christ Lord, give in to him daily, break down our sinful resistance and submit our wills to him. It was earnest, sincere, and depressing.

The period ended with the hymn

> Take my life, and let it be
> Consecrated, Lord, to thee.

That also depressed me, partly because it was played so slowly and sung so droningly and partly because most people don't really mean it. Suddenly I remembered that one minister, in announcing that hymn, said they would omit the fourth verse as the congregation obviously didn't mean it. That verse? "Take my silver and my gold, not a mite would I withhold." I chuckled to myself at the memory.

Then I realized that I had once done exactly what the omitted verse said. Before a minister and a congregation I had pledged loud and clear, "With all my worldly goods I thee endow."

That didn't cover very much, really. After the wedding and until my next paycheck I had only enough to see us through the month and allow three days at a hotel. Through the years the money hasn't been my money or her money, but our money. And you know, neither of us seems to have suffered very much.

That memory started me thinking about the devotional address, and I discovered why it depressed me. It was all about sacrifice, giving in, submission.

I wondered how it would sound at weddings if we told the two people all they would have to put up with: dishes to wash, socks to darn, diapers to change, grass to cut, furnaces to stoke. Then we would add the horrible warning that they would have to put up with each other, day after day, for fifty years or so.

But in marriage isn't that exactly what they are looking forward to? That's why they are getting married. You won't scare a bride by telling her about all the housework ahead; you'll just attract her. And you won't scare him off by telling him he'll have to live with her. Isn't that what both of them want?

Shouldn't the same thing be true of religion? Unfortunately we've gotten it the other way around. We tell people of the requirements, conditions, and burdens and imply that they'll find it hard and won't like it, but that if they want to get to heaven they'll have to do it. Then we imply, if we don't say it right out, that when they get to heaven, having earned it by their resignation, sacrifice, and submission, they will find all those unpleasant things over and done with.

We're wrong. What we were describing *is* heaven, just as housework and living together *is* marriage, granted that one essential requirement—love.

In one meeting we were discussing love, that state of mind and heart so difficult to define. Suddenly I had a flash of inspiration. "Love," I said, "is what enables two people to live together." Think how impossible, indeed how terrible, it would be to be condemned to spend even one, year, much less fifty years, with many people we know in hour-after-hour and day-after-day association. Yet that is what we do in marriage—what we choose to do—and we don't find it terrible at all. Indeed the prospect intrigues the prospective couple. That is because of love, and only when love withers and dies does the association become unbearable.

Does the idea of making Christ Lord, submitting to him and living in constant companionship with him, seem like a burden? If so, then we haven't the right to try it at all, any more than we have the right to get married if the prospect of living and working together and sharing all things in common seems like a burden.

Having made that vow many years ago, "with all my worldly goods I thee endow," my wife and I have had a lot of fun sharing what we have, and often what we haven't. So singing that omitted verse, "Take my silver and my gold," can be fun too, for it not only means *giving to* Christ but also *sharing with* Christ.

And the secret to the joy of both is in one word, love.

SORRY, GOD,
I DIDN'T KNOW IT WAS YOU

A class at school, discussing the death of Christ, said it was the most terrible crime ever committed. They were horrified when I said I didn't agree. "Wasn't it killing God?" they asked. My answer confused them even more: "Why should killing God be worse than killing anyone else?"

Well, why should it?

On Good Friday in many churches people watch, in a sense, by the cross of Christ until that anguished cry, "My God, my God, why hast thou forsaken me?" and the last whisper, "Father, into thy hands I commend my spirit." For two thousand years that has been going on, a long, long time to remember anyone's death and to keep talking about one act of cruelty and injustice.

Yes, one act. One, out of thousands, yes, even millions. One cross out of the many hundreds Rome erected in Palestine. There were two others on that hill on that same day. But this one was different, people say. The others who were crucified were just ordinary people, but this was the Son of God. To all the other crimes through the ages, men added this one—they crucified the Son of God. That is what men say. I wonder how God looks at it.

In the parable about the last judgment Jesus said he would judge all nations using only one formula, whether men had fed him when he was hungry, clothed him when he was naked, and visited him when he was sick or in prison. The judged would exclaim with one voice that never, never had they seen him hungry, naked, thirsty, sick, or in prison. Then Jesus would answer, "Inasmuch as ye have done it [or have done it not]unto one of the least of these my brethren, ye have done it [or have done it not] unto me" (Matt. 25:40).

That is the answer I have to take to Calvary. There I don't see one cross only but all the crosses, not on one day only but on all the days of all the years. Jesus' parable demands that of me.

That surely puts an end to the terrible accusation that it was the Jews alone who killed Jesus. Our forefathers thought this justified their herding all the Jews into ghettos, spitting on them, robbing them and killing them. Did the Jews kill Jesus? From one viewpoint yes, *and so did we*. They are still killing him, *and so are we*. Inasmuch as we have done it to the least of men we have done it to Jesus. Whenever one innocent person has been jailed, robbed, or killed, whenever injustice has been done to the least of men, it has been done to God. Good Friday speaks not of just one cross or one death but millions of them. Perhaps it takes Good Friday to make us see all the other crosses and the accusation against one race to make us see the finger pointed at us and at all races.

It is important to see that. The cross of Christ has for two thousand years been the symbol of forgiveness. But before forgiveness there has to be the recognition of guilt and the determination that, God helping us, it shall never happen again.

Happen again! Is that possible? If Jesus came back to earth would men crucify him again? No, perhaps not. We have more modern and efficient methods of destruction now. We might use an atomic explosion or perhaps a blockbuster bomb (is there really so much difference?) or a speeding automobile. It could be in Vietnam or alongside the Suez Canal or on a highway in Ontario or on a street in New York. Does it matter so much whether it happens on a cross, under a bomb, or in a motor car?

It may be, however, that Jesus is less concerned than we think about his cross. After all, in his parable about the judgment he didn't mention it. He didn't condemn men for killing him but because they hadn't fed, clothed, or visited him in his distress. Perhaps if we were more concerned about all the hungry, thirsty, ragged, sick, and imprisoned of the world, if we heard the cries of the distressed and lonely, the persecuted and the suffering, there would be fewer crosses and less flaring injustice to worry about.

When Good Friday comes, let us spare a moment from watching at the cross of Jesus to look at all the unfortunates of the world. If we don't know where to look, then just let our eyes follow where his are looking. There we will see them, and seeing them, we will find him too.

GOD AND OUR FELLOWS

When our cat was having her first family, it created a problem for her. She is a friendly cat, and a talkative one. In fact she talks all the time, preferably to us. Not that we understand her, but that doesn't seem to make any difference. As long as she can talk, that is all that matters. Being with us wherever we were and talking to us was once her life. Then came her first family and her problem.

She had to be with her family—it was both a duty and a pleasure. But how could she be with them and us too, or talk to us and them too? Though her family seemed not to understand her conversation either or pay much attention to it, she still talked.

When the kittens were six weeks old we found a home for one, the biggest and greediest of the litter. We found that though three were left Josephine could count. She said so mournfully, reproachfully, and incessantly. She missed her kitten, and apparently she missed us too.

When the kittens became more independent, Josephine spent more time with us, sitting on the chesterfield while we watched TV, on the table when we tried to write letters, and on the nearest chair while we ate our meals. But hers was restless company, for the kittens were still on her mind. She wanted their company as well as ours.

The night her kitten left home Josephine spent ten minutes or so with us on the chesterfield. Then suddenly she left, chattering away. From the kitchen we heard more chattering, solicitous and encouraging, and into the living room marched four cats, Josephine and her brood. She led them to the chesterfield, chatting gaily, and was completely happy again.

I suppose in some sense we are like gods to Josephine; we feed her, take care of her, and provide company for her. That is flattering to us, but gods, no matter how beneficent and adored, don't quite make up for one's own kind, especially one's family. That was Josephine's problem.

It is our problem too. No matter how beneficent and adored our God may be, he is not enough by himself. We also need our own kind. Cats and people are not so different after all.

Have you ever thought how people and God are mixed up together in Christian history? All through there is a twofold relationship—between the worshiper and God and the worshiper and his fellows. Neither relationship is enough by itself. Alone, each is unbalanced, unnatural, and false.

But isn't religion the worship of God? Yes, in a sense that is what it is. But some also declare that religion is the service of mankind, doing our best to be kindly, generous, honest, and giving our lives to help others. Yes, it is that too. Yet it is neither one alone. It is both together.

Jesus, when asked what was the first commandment, answered by giving two and combining them. "Thou shalt love the Lord thy God . . . and thy neighbour as thyself." There it is again, people and God, God and people.

A rather bleak individual once told me he didn't like going to church but preferred to worship on the hills, alone with God. It didn't seem to have done him much good, for he was bleak in manner and bleak in outlook. Yes, of course. Turning to God alone makes for bleakness, like Mount Sinai, cold and forbidding. Yet turning to men alone is even more bleak and lonely, lacking the source of power, patience, hope, and love. In fact, each alone is a religion of despair. Like Josephine we need both, God and our own kind, our own kind and God.

How wonderful that it should be so! One verse which has cheered and comforted me is about the time of our departure from this life. That is a frightening prospect for many of us, and though we are convinced that we shall then meet God in Christ it is cold and dark. But listen to what Paul said, "those who sleep in him will the Lord bring with him when he comes." Those who have gone before, those whom we, in John Henry Newman's words, "have loved long since and lost awhile" will be there, smiling at us, welcoming us.

For heaven, the goal of religion and the goal of

all worship, again brings together the two, God and people, people and God. It is only when this happens here or in heaven, that we can really share and enjoy the presence of God.

PLAYING IT THROUGH

Do you watch football games? Are you even faintly interested in them? I do, and I'm interested, more than a little. But then I used to play football once upon a time.

I remember a game years ago when my alma mater was playing its greatest rival. Had my team won, they would have been champions. The playing field was in a terrible condition, half-covered with water. Indeed some students rowed a boat around part of it during half time. My team showed quite clearly that they didn't like the water. The tacklers waited at the edge of the field for the runners to come out to them, and the halfbacks stood at the edge too, waiting for the ball to bounce to them. But the other team didn't seem to notice the water. They plowed through it like submarines and dashed through it like tanks. The result was obvious. My team lost.

After the game I happened to be at the station as the losing team waited dismally to go home. I commiserated with one player about the loss, and he answered, "The worst of it is, we'll have to play again."

That horrified me. I played football for fun. I liked it, couldn't get enough of it. The end of the season came all too soon for me. Sure I got bumped and bruised; my nose was twisted out of shape several times; and after each game I would ache and limp. That was all part of the fun. And here was a player who had gone so much farther than I (I only reached junior ranks) lamenting that he had to play again.

But then there is a good deal of that kind of thing around, isn't there? A common attitude seems to be, "Stop the world, I want to get off." So many young people are beatniks, and so many older ones seem to want to quit. Apparently the ultimate tragedy to them is that they have to keep on playing and living. They echo in their way the words of the football player, "The worst of it is, we'll have to play again."

Christianity used to be like that too in some of its expressions. Running through many hymns was the longing for eternal rest, to be wafted up to heaven "on flowery beds of ease." The goal was to get done with the rough-and-tumble of life, its blows and battles, and to sit around on clouds, playing harps and doing nothing at all. Perhaps because I'm too heavy for a cloud and can't play a harp, that doesn't appeal to me. But that isn't Christianity, never was, and never will be, any more than the football player's comment was football.

When I heard him I thought, "No wonder you lost, and you'll lose again next time." Which of course they did. That attitude always brings defeat, in football, in life, or in Christianity.

All three should be games we long to play, can't get enough of, and the rougher and tougher the going the more we should revel in it. That is how I read the tenth chapter of Matthew. Jesus in commissioning the disciples warned them of the dangers and difficulties ahead and called them to faith and endurance.

Life is a game to be played out, not a soft, easy, safe refuge from the storms of life. Christianity is facing odds, confronting enemies, and taking up one's cross, not with resignation but with defiant enthusiasm.

Of course by nature we are easily scared, our hearts beat anxiously, and our knees shake. Mine do. So do any honest man's. But Christ is there to urge us on, despite what our knees do. Christianity calls to us find our manhood and to go on no matter how afraid we are. And haven't our finest hours been when we did dare the difficult and dangerous, spurning safety and ease, battled against the odds, and won?

One of Robert Browning's poems has come back to me again and again since first I read it in high school. It is called "Prospice" and it seems to me to echo the Christian challenge like a trumpet blast, especially these lines:

I would hate that death bandaged my eyes, and
    forebore,
    And bade me creep past.
No! let me taste the whole of it, fare like my peers
    The heroes of old,
Bear the brunt, in a minute pay glad life's arrears
    Of pain, darkness, and cold.
For sudden the worst turns the best to the brave.

THE BLACK HARBINGER

The crow is a most unfortunate bird. He has a
voice like a sea gull with a sore throat, and the
more he tries to pour out glorious music the harsher
he sounds. Yet there is one time when I wait anxiously for the cawing of the crows, hoarse and
unmusical though it is, and thrill when I hear it.
That is when winter seems endless.

Where crows go during the coldest months I
don't know, but anyway they aren't around this
part of Ontario. Then near the end of February
or the beginning of March, when the snow is still
deep on the ground and the winds blow directly
from the North Pole, there'll come a far-off cawing.
Flapping to the evergreens around the cemetery the
crows announce their presence again.

Even the sparrows haven't been around, and the
pair who nest annually under the eaves of the
pump house haven't been seen for months. Winter

has apparently discouraged them as by the end of February it has discouraged me. Then when winter seems to be going on forever, there comes the hoarse, raucous cawing of the crows and I take heart. Spring is coming. The crows say so, and Mr. and Mrs. Sparrow will come soon to inspect last year's nest and wonder what to do about it.

Everyone else looks for the first robin, the first crocus, the first snowdrop, or the first budding of the forsythia, but I look for the crows. All these others come when winter is almost over, when even I know that spring is just around the corner. But God bless the crows, they shout their triumphant if noisy greeting before there is any other indication of spring.

Thinking of the crows I remembered a retired schoolteacher in my first church years ago. She had come from New England to keep house for her bachelor brother, and her voice betrayed her origin. To say she wasn't musical was an understatement. Whether she *could* sing or not I don't know, but I do know she never did. She stood silently, prim and rather formidable, during all the hymns. I remember her particularly because I tried to get her brother interested in religion, in the church—or just plain interested. He was polite, evasive, and discouraging. He, to my knowledge, had never darkened a church door.

Then some years later I went back to the church to preach at an anniversary long after my spinster schoolteacher friend had died. To my amazement

I found her brother a most devout and sincere Christian, a faithful churchgoer and one of the pillars of the church. How did it happen? After his sister died the brother yielded to an influence he had never acknowledged during her lifetime.

Do you see the connection between my spinster friend and the crows? As the crows with their hoarse voices are the harbingers of spring, so she in her way was the harbinger of a spiritual spring for her brother. My one regret was that she hadn't lived to see how he had responded.

I think of another person, a young girl who, after some years of illness, died from cancer of the liver at the age of twenty. As I think of her I remember her yellowness, her extreme thinness, and her weakness. But most of all I remember her eyes lighting up, the smile on her lips, and her words as, two weeks before she died, she said quite naturally, "I can't understand how anyone can help loving Jesus Christ." That was the sure proclamation of spring in the very depths of winter.

I suppose most of us wish we could sing like robins or had the beauty of the crocus, and most certainly we all want to live in the warmth and brightness of spring. What grand work we could do then! What we forget is that in the profusion of robins and crocuses, in all the burgeoning life of spring, people get callous. The message becomes commonplace and is taken for granted. It is the crows in the snow who most triumphantly proclaim spring's coming.

We forget too that the most triumphant proclamation of Christ is not in the eloquence of great preachers or the music of the finest choirs, but in the faithful, steadfast, undaunted living of ordinary people in the depths of their own bleak wintertime.

CROWS—AND SOME CHRISTIANS

Now that I have said a good word about crows I'm sorry I did. I've gotten fed up with crows. When I congratulated the crows for arriving in Ontario in the height of winter and proclaiming the coming of spring, I didn't know that they'd arrive in our own back yard and become nuisances.

They haunt the maple trees to the south of the property and watch for the cat. The moment she appears from the barn in the morning they greet her with raucous insults and what, I am sure, are the most horrible swearwords. They hop to the lowest branches, flop down to the slender walnut tree, flap their wings and shout. The cat doesn't mind it so much now, though at first she was quite timid, but *we* mind. After all, five o'clock in the morning is no time to listen to crows. Indeed no time of day is a good time to be deafened by hoarse, raucous cawing within fifty feet of the house. I wish the crows would go away, a long, long distance away, and stay there.

47

Crows have been likened to ministers. Perhaps one reason is they are both clothed in sober black, an even more dismal color than clerical gray. Another reason may be their constant scolding and the infuriating superiority they show toward cats, people, and everything else. I've never seen any person or thing more self-righteous or more hypocritical than a crow. And, come to think of it, when I mentioned them before as being harbingers of spring, it was early March and we all knew that it wasn't really spring by a long way. Hypocrites is right!

Of course, some people think ministers are hypocrites too, an unfortunate fact we ministers might as well face and accept. But then people resisting Christianity and the claims of Christ are apt to think all Christians are hypocrites, a fact we Christians must accept and indeed must try to do something about. To the unrepentant and unregenerate, conduct more righteous than their own always smacks of self-righteousness and hypocrisy, a silent and unbearable criticism of their own conduct.

Made as we are, it is difficult to keep from seeming self-righteous, and often, I'm afraid, actually being it. And it is just as difficult for ministers to keep from preaching, which to the popular mind is scolding and criticism—crows screaming at the cat. Unfortunately, often that is what it is.

Have you ever noticed the difference between the prophets and Jesus? The prophets make gloomy reading, for me at least. They were always prophesying doom, blasting people for their sins, and calling down the wrath of God upon them. Certainly it was deserved, but that didn't make it any easier to take—or, nowadays, to read.

Jesus, on the other hand, didn't blast everyone, like fiery John the Baptist did. He spoke in simple language of a heavenly Father, of forgiveness, love, and righteousness. He healed people who didn't deserve it. He comforted and cheered the unfortunate. The worst condemnation heard from his lips was against the self-righteous, the people who boasted of their own goodness and shouted against everyone else—like crows!

I've wondered a lot lately about sins, my own and other people's. Should I point out iniquities, proclaim judgment, and put the fear of God into sinners? Then I've thought of the crows. I hear them shouting and cursing in the maple trees and realize how little they accomplish. Even the cat has ceased to be terrified by them. How little, too, the ranting of people has accomplished.

One morning I heard two songs, the crows' and a cardinal's. In imagination that morning I listened in my mind to two people, John the Baptist and Jesus. It seemed to me that if people will not hear, believe, and accept the message of love Jesus spoke, then John the Baptist won't touch them at all. When people don't thrill to the song of the cardinal, the crows will scold in vain.

INHERITED RELIGION

A Scotsman and an Irishman were having an argument. The Irishman shouted in exasperation, "An Irishman I was born, and an Irishman I will die!" "Man," replied the Scotsman pityingly, "have you no ambition?"

You can make that story fit any nationality you like, or even a political persuasion or religion. For as John Kieran wrote in his book *Not Under Oath*, "Most of us come by our politics the same way we come by our religion—we inherit it."

It is peculiar, isn't it, that we so often boast of the very things for which we personally are not responsible at all. That is the crux of the race problem. We were born white, black, yellow, or brown. We ourselves had nothing to do with it. It was, if you like, sheer accident, the accident of inheritance. So why we should boast about what we are and look down on others is almost beyond comprehension.

It is true of politics also for probably the majority of people. I remember one election when I was eleven and in public school. I was quite innocent about politics and was quite bewildered when the boys in the school yard shouted for one party or the other. I was left out in the cold till I could ask

Father at noon, "Father, are we Grits or Tories?" Back at school I joined in the fray with a heat and enthusiasm unequaled by any. I confess, rather shamefacedly, that I still lean toward that inherited political party. I guess John Kieran was right.

The worst part of Kieran's statement, though, was that he said we come by our religion through inheritance also, and I'm afraid that is all too true. It is the worst part because religion should be the search for truth, the ultimate truth, the truth which alone can provide the solutions for problems of race, nationality, and politics—yes, and all the other problems of the world too.

It is a fairly common statement and an idea shared by far too many people that one religion is as good as another. That idea is as silly as to say that the science of any period is as good as that of any other, that the science of the fifth or seventeenth century is as good as the science of today. Science is the search for truth, a developing and unfolding truth, and religion should be even more than science the search for truth and the discovery of it. Any generation which cannot make new discoveries is a generation in danger of losing the very truth it has inherited.

But besides being an understanding of and a search for God, the source of all truth, religion is personal. In the Old Testament the words "the God of Abraham, of Isaac, and of Jacob, the God of your fathers" frequently appear. But how limited it would be and how ignorant we would be if that was all the religion we had! What our forefathers discovered is a valuable step on the road to our own discovery of God. Their discoveries had meaning for the men of that day, but they are not enough for us now. The discoveries of others are of no value unless we make them ours and use them as stepping stones to wider, greater truths opening out before us.

John Kieran said that we inherited our religion. There is real value to an inheritance, provided it is an incentive and not a goal. Sometimes a mistaken loyalty makes us boast of the race, nationality, politics, or religion of our ancestors. Unfortunately this boasting is too often the most fanatical of all, and the most retrograde. It has been responsible for more persecutions and more wars than almost any other cause. Let us give thanks for our inheritance, be grateful for what our fathers strove after and discovered. But we must go on from there. Our primary loyalty is not to the past, not to any inheritance of race, nationality, or creed, but to the truth.

Only as we are loyal to the truth, as we cherish that which we have found, and as we keep seeking for further and fuller truth, can that truth become our own and set us free.

PICNICKING WITH GOD

The play *Green Pastures* and the book *Ol' Man Adam and His Chillun* both open with a picnic in heaven. The angels, archangels, cherubs, and the Lawd God are having a fish fry. They run out of firmament (some kind of syrup I suppose), and the Lawd God on request r'ars back, as he says, and passes a miracle. He produces so much firmament that he has to create a world for it to run off into. And that, so the play and the book say, is how the world began.

I suppose many people may be a bit shocked about the scene. Do angels go on picnics? Does the Lord God attend a fish fry, and does he smoke ten-cent "seegars"? It sounds faintly blasphemous, to say the least. But I wonder if it would ever occur to us that this folksy picture, ten-cent seegar and all, may be nearer the real truth than our own strait-laced idea.

Perhaps we might say that this is simply a matter of opinion without any facts to support either view. The fiercest quarrels and bitterest arguments center around such unsupported differences. But this isn't unsupported. The facts are there, easily discovered and beyond dispute, and the *Green Pastures* version has the facts, including the picture of the Lord God as a darkskinned individual.

First of all, Jesus was a Palestinian Jew, an Oriental, an outdoorsman, black-haired, brown-eyed, and with a dark skin. Second, the last incident John records about Jesus occurred after he had risen. He dropped in on the disciples at the Sea of Galilee and prepared a fish fry for them, a picnic beside the lake. (John 21:9-12)

Third, about that "seegar"—*Green Pastures* missed the boat a little there (they hadn't any seegars in Jesus' day). But Jesus did drink wine, and we can't quibble that it was really unfermented grape juice. It was wine. The Pharisees called Jesus a man gluttonous, a winebibber, a friend of publicans and sinners.

The play was right then in two-and-a half out of the three points. But most of all it was right in the fundamental picture. It showed heaven, or religion, or being with God, as a pleasant, informal, and wholly delightful experience. That was the way it was with Jesus and the apostles in the Gospels. *Green Pastures* and the Gospels share the same atmosphere and give the same picture of God.

Imagine going on a fish fry with God! Personally it doesn't appeal to me, I don't like fish. (Maybe God would provide a hamburger for me.) However, it isn't the kind of food, it is the company, the fun, and the relaxing, pleasurable experience. If only religion could really be that kind of thing!

It was once, if the Gospels are true. It was for Jesus and the twelve, for the five thousand beside the Sea of Galilee, for the disciples after Jesus had risen.

What a wonderful memory the disciples had of their last time with Jesus shortly before he ascended to the very throne of God! They sat around a campfire, nibbled at bits of the fish which he had cooked, picked the bones out of their mouths with their fingers, and exchanged smiles with God himself.

If only that kind of experience could be ours!

Well, why can't it? If we believe that Jesus does really forgive and forget, if we believe what John wrote about that marvelous picnic, then today might be a picnic with God for us too.

THE TERRIBLE TEPID

Which of the modern inventions and improvements is the most valuable is a real question, but there is one for which I breathe a sigh of relief whenever I think of it—the automatic furnace. No more shoveling coal, sifting ashes, adjusting drafts, and having the basement filled with coal dust! It makes me tired even to think of it.

From my teens on I played nursemaid to a coal furnace for seven months or more each year and hated every bit of it. There may be some jobs which grow on you, even though they are arduous and dirty, but tending a coal furnace isn't one of them.

It was spring when I thought of this, a peculiar time of year apparently, for one would think that January, when the temperature drops to zero and the furnace goes full blast, would be a more logical time. In the spring the air is balmy, more or less, and you might think the furnace could be forgotten down in the basement. But not so, not if it is a coal furnace. It would either be going too hard, making the house unbearably hot, or it would be out, leaving the house cold and clammy. How many times in spring and fall mine went out is past counting. I could keep it going pretty well in winter simply by adjusting the drafts, and putting on lots of coal, but in spring or fall it was beyond me. Either too hot or completely out, that was its way— and it always seemed to be going out. Then I'd have to get wood and paper, rake out the coals and cinders, and start all over again. So that is why in spring particularly I thank God for automatic furnaces.

Thinking of coal furnaces reminded me of a verse from the Revelation, where Jesus said to Laodicea, "Because thou art lukewarm, and neither cold nor hot, I will spew thee out of my mouth." It reminded me of furnaces because when the furnace fire became lukewarm, I knew it would go out despite all I could do. Perhaps Jesus, looking at that lukewarm church, knew it was going out too.

It may seem shocking to hear Jesus say that he wished a church (and that also means Christians) was either hot or cold. Does Jesus really prefer a person who never darkens a church door to one who goes, say, every four or five months? Does he prefer an out-and-out pagan to a nominal Christian? That is what the verse seems to indicate. The lukewarm church and the lukewarm people of Laodicea were not just going to go out by themselves. Jesus said he would spit them out of his mouth in supreme disgust. Apparently they were an affront to him and a handicap to his cause.

The clue is in the words "a handicap to his cause." The book of the Revelation is the account of a warfare in which Christ and the church were engaged against all the power of Rome. There were sufferings, persecutions and martyrdoms. For centuries it seemed as though the church and Christianity must go down to defeat and be wiped out. In that warfare, as in all warfare, the greatest handicap wasn't the out-and-out enemy, but the lukewarm ally.

We are told that when each persecution started, about nine tenths of the so-called Christians would hurry to the nearest magistrate to recant. They said they never meant it, they had never really belonged, and that they would worship the emperor or do anything at all to avoid prison or death. Then came the persecutions, the crucifixions, and Christians thrown to the wild beasts in the arena. What a contrast that presented to the avowed enemies of Christianity—the lukewarm running for shelter while the real Christians suffered the horrors of the persecution. How they must have scorned all Christians because of the lukewarm.

Yet when many of those enemies saw the courage, faith, and character of the martyrs, they admired, envied, and sought to join them. When the persecutions were over, the church was ten times stronger than it had been at the beginning, despite the desertions of the lukewarm.

That warfare is still going on. The business of the church is not primarily to enlist candidates for heaven but soldiers for Christ. Make no mistake— his army isn't playing at war. It is not easy to stand against a new and popular morality, to hold fast to Christian principles in business, to fight against smut and filth and remain decent and understanding, and, above all, to love our enemies. In *that* warfare the lukewarm are still the greatest handicap.

BIRTH NOTICES OF THE GREAT

A facetious correspondent sent a letter to a university magazine complaining that, while he noted frequent accounts of the deaths of great men, he failed to find any references to a more important subject, the births of great men! He had something, hadn't he? The great men who have died have finished any contribution they could make, but the needs of the world are just as great as ever, and who is going to carry on their work?

That is what we'd all like to know. It would be heartening if it were possible to have birth notices such as, "At Epworth rectory, Lincolnshire, on June 28th, 1703, to the Rev. Samuel Wesley and Susanna Wesley, a son, John, their fifteenth child. This is one of the most important births to take place in centuries. This infant will change the face of England, save it from bloody revolution, and almost unaided revitalize Christianity throughout the world."

Had such a notice appeared, imagine the pilgrimages to the little village of Epworth to gaze on the face of that baby destined to be such an important force in the world. Of course there wasn't any such notice. I imagine that having had fourteen other children the Wesleys didn't even put a comment in the parish magazine, supposing there was one. The correspondent who complained about the omission of references to the births of great men was asking the impossible.

Or was it really impossible? Sometimes coming events do cast their shadows before. There were Simeon and Anna waiting in the temple at Jerusalem for the promise of the Lord's Christ. There were the shepherds and the wise men making their pilgrimage to the manger to gaze on the baby who, long after they were dead, would change the whole course of history.

Sometimes to a baby himself, almost before he

can think or understand, there comes a foretelling of great purposes and a divine commission. So it was with Jeremiah, who heard the voice which whispered so insistently, "Before I formed you in the womb I knew you, and before you were born I consecrated you; I appointed you a prophet to the nations" (Jer. 1:5 RSV).

It would be a great comfort in times of world stress and turmoil, when everything seems to be going to pieces and there is no hope, if we could be told that an infant born in some remote village would save civilization. Even if that revelation were denied to the world, it would be almost as great a comfort if the infant himself knew his destiny, as John the Baptist knew, and Jeremiah and Jesus. Or would it be a comfort? We remember the sufferings of Jeremiah, that John the Baptist was beheaded and Jesus crucified. So perhaps the babies so informed of their destinies might be tempted to complain with Hamlet,

> The time is out of joint; O cursèd spite,
> That ever I was born to set it right!

While no newspaper can tell us in its birth notices of those destined to set the world aright, and few who are to change the world know ahead of time the labor, the glory, and the penalties which lie in store for them, there is something of which we can be certain. In the past the world has never lacked for men to lead it in times of apparent disaster, and the probablity is that it never will. If we believe in the God who selected Jeremiah before he was born, planned for centuries for the coming of Jesus, and has had his chosen instruments through all the ages, then surely the future is safe with him. Already in a cradle in some obscure village may lie a baby who will lead the world out of its present darkness. Who it is, we do not and cannot know. But we do know God.

And if we know God, surely we know that it is not only those specially appointed agents, those future great men, whom he chooses. There is a multitude who will prepare the way for them, a multitude whose unheralded labor and faithful service will make possible what the great are to accomplish. They also are the chosen of God.

So let's stop worrying about the birth of great men and simply consider ourselves and the task committed to us. Let us believe that even in obscurity we are chosen of God to prepare the way for great men to come and to lay foundations on which they can build.

WAITING

Rudyard Kipling wrote a "counsel of perfection" entitled "If." Most everyone is familiar with it, as it is generally taught to the young who, being innocent, aren't aware that the *ifs* are about as impossible to follow as anything man has thought up.

Every admonition, though, makes good sense (possibly that is why admonitions are so difficult) but to my mind what makes the best sense and is the most difficult to follow is, "If you can wait and not be tired by waiting." I suppose I picked this line for emphasis because for me waiting has always been a wearying and difficult business. Perhaps it is true also for you and for most everyone else.

It would be difficult enough if it were simply waiting, but it is waiting *in faith,* waiting with a conviction that the tide will turn, that the final outcome will be victory. And it is also waiting without a time limit, with no outward indication of any lightening of the skies. And most desperate of all, it is waiting when everyone else seems to have given you up. Yes, "If you can wait and not be tired by waiting."

I look back on several occasions when all I could do, apparently, was wait. The most anxious and desperate time of all was some twenty years ago when the waiting extended over eighteen months and seemed endless. To believe then with Pippa in Browning's poem that "God's in his heaven—all's right with the world," was a denial of common sense. To believe that any road went on, much less the desired road, seemed an impossibility. At times my spirit almost gave out, but never entirely, thank God. For from that year and a half of desperation has come, I think, anything of value that I've done.

The road did go on again, an upward road, and again and again I thank God for the grace to wait it through.

It wasn't Kipling alone who counseled waiting. The psalmist did too. "Wait on the Lord," he wrote, "be of good courage, and he shall strengthen thine heart: Wait, I say, on the Lord."

And Isaiah did. "Even the youths shall faint and be weary, and the young men shall utterly fall: but they that wait upon the Lord shall renew their strength; they shall mount up with wings as eagles; they shall run, and not be weary; and they shall walk, and not faint."

In Luke 24 Jesus commanded his disciples to wait. "Tarry ye in Jerusalem," he told them just before his ascension, "until ye be endued with power from on high." And again in Acts 1, "Wait for the promise of the Father."

Perhaps it seems that the counsel to wait and not be weary means simply to develop endurance, to learn to tide over the doldrums which often come to men just as they used to come to sailing ships. Or we may think that it is to test our faith and maybe even to develop and enrich it. But I'd like to add the experience of Habakkuk to the words of the psalmist and Isaiah, and emphasize not "wait," but "on the Lord." Habakkuk sought a word from God. He took his stand on the watchtower and to him the word came: "The vision is yet for an appointed time; . . . though it tarry, wait for it."

The problem isn't simply waiting, and it certainly

isn't waiting on God in the sense of trying to make him move faster or in the direction we want. Rather it is waiting *for* God. It is, as Jesus told the disciples, waiting for the promise of the Father. It is waiting for a new direction in life, a new power for life, a new goal, incentive, vision. For many that is the greatest need today. Too often we are like the man in the *Nonsense Novels* who "flung himself from the room, flung himself upon his horse and rode madly off in all directions."

Perhaps you yourself are in a time of waiting. If so, thank God, take heart, and wait on him. The road may have seemed to have stopped, not just for the time being but for good. In God's time it will go on again, no longer your road but his. And that is worth waiting for.

CRITICIZING GOD

Did you ever feel like criticizing God? No? Well, I must say you are a very unusual person—and besides I don't think you are being entirely honest. If I had a dollar for every person I've heard saying, "Why did God do this, or permit it to be done?" I'd be rich. And if I had a quarter for every time people have felt like asking that question, I'd be a millionaire.

Some people may think such questions are blasphemy which God will punish severely and which threaten to destroy religion. However, such critics are not the danger to religion they may suppose. In fact, the opposite is true. Religion owes more to the questioners, critics, yes, and the doubters, than to anything else.

Think for a moment. If it weren't for such people we'd still be worshiping hideous idols, the promiscuous deities of Olympus, or the Roman emperors. It is because people dared to question, criticize, and doubt that some of the darkness has been banished and some light has come. So if you are inwardly disturbed, if you feel like questioning and criticizing, take heart. It may be that you are on the way from darkness to light.

But we need to be careful. Not all questioners and doubters have helped either themselves or the world. When the questions are selfish and the doubts inspired by rebellion, then they are a snare and a delusion and lead only to deeper darkness. There must be a desire to find truth, no matter where it leads or what it costs. Above all there must be a standard by which we judge, so that we are forced to say, "The eternal God must be perfection itself, otherwise he is not God. If what I see does not seem to meet that standard, then, so far as my human understanding goes, it is wrong."

In the fifth chapter of Matthew that is what Jesus did. He looked at the old traditions—for instance "an eye for an eye, and a tooth for a tooth"—and declared they weren't good enough. Loving your neighbors and hating your enemies wasn't good enough either. "Be ye therefore perfect," Jesus said, "even as your Father which is in heaven is perfect." Jesus was saying that his ideals and standards were higher than those age-old commandments and revealed more of God than men knew in those far-off days. God must be greater "than the measure of man's mind."

In Isaiah, God declares, "My thoughts are not your thoughts, neither are your ways my ways, . . . for as the heavens are higher than the earth, so are my ways higher than your ways, and my thoughts than your thoughts." Take the highest that men have reached, their loftiest thoughts and greatest ideals—they still fall far short of God. If the picture men have given of God, or your own picture of him, falls short of that standard, it is wrong.

Next to Jesus the prophets were the most severe critics of what men declared God was like. Hosea made one of the greatest discoveries. His wife became promiscuous and left him and their children. Sick at heart and hating the evil in her, Hosea still loved her. He knew she wasn't all bad and knew that she could be greater than she had proved herself. So he bought her back from her harlotry and installed her in his home as housekeeper, and later on restored her as his wife in truth. Then he reasoned that if a man could have such compassion and understanding and could make such a sacrifice, God could not be less.

No, God cannot be less—less than men's love,

justice, sacrifice, hope, patience, faith, goodness. God must be greater—far, far greater. In our ideals and hopes we have set a standard not only for ourselves but for God. All that men have taught, thought, had handed down in tradition or been told to accept on faith which falls short of the highest ideals and loftiest standards is false. It is not God who has fallen short but our picture of him, and we ourselves who have fallen short of God.

Again we must take care. Our standards and our ideals are often faulty. Selfishness may creep in, and our criticism come from rebellion. It isn't our criticism, questioning, or even doubts which are wrong; it is the motives from which they spring. But if earnestly and sincerely we seek to find God, then surely, though slowly, he will reveal himself to us. For it is still true today as it was for Jeremiah, "Ye shall seek for me and ye shall find me, saith the Lord, when ye search after me with all your hearts."

EASTER? SO WHAT?

The first Easter and the present one are much alike in three respects.

On that morning the women went early to the sepulchre, found the stone rolled away, saw a vision of angels, and came running back crying that Jesus was risen.

The disciples heard them but didn't believe them. "You know what women are like," they probably said to each other. "Their words seemed to them as idle tales."

Those two reactions are evident today too—some people loudly proclaim that Jesus is alive while others pooh-pooh the idea. It's always happening.

The third reaction is far more serious. Two people were going home to Emmaus. They had heard the stories, listened to the women, seen the disbelief of the disciples, and decided that to them the whole thing couldn't matter less. "So what?" describes their attitude. "We trusted," they said, "that it had been he which should have redeemed Israel." So what did it matter whether Jesus was risen or not? What they had followed him for could no longer be done. For their purpose a risen Jesus was as useless as a dead one.

It is that third reaction, the "so what?" that is still the predominant one. The first question isn't really whether or not he is alive but what difference it makes. Until we answer that, we will have no real conviction about the resurrection and, what is more important, no power in it. That is what Paul wanted to discover for himself. "That I may know him, and the power of his resurrection," he wrote to the Philippians. Paul was right; it is the power that counts, what the resurrection can do with people.

If we are honest, we know that there is a lot of life on which the resurrection has not only no bearing but to which it is a real handicap. It didn't mean a thing to the restoration of Israel, as the two going to Emmaus realized. It doesn't mean a thing to any earthly kingdom, any amassing of wealth, any personal enrichment, any advancement of our personal ambitions. For such things Jesus dead or Jesus alive couldn't matter less. It is right here that true Christianity and the risen Jesus meet their stiffest opposition and find their chief enemies. For where men's purposes are selfish, earthly, and material Christianity is a handicap, and the risen Christ an affront. Some may argue about whether he is risen or not but most of us, when he makes no contribution to our own personal gain, simply shrug and say, "So what?"

What was discovered by the disciples, including the two materialists going home to Emmaus, was that their emphasis had been on the wrong word, *risen* instead of *Jesus*. It was *Jesus* who was risen, their friend, the one who loved them and whom they loved, the one who told them of God. It was *Jesus* who was alive. Until we learn to make that same emphasis, we'll never find the real meaning of Easter. We must discover Jesus first and learn to love him. When we have done that, the resurrection becomes not just a fact (or perhaps not a fact) but the greatest and most wonderful thing that ever happened.

I came across a comment in a detective story.

The detective, not a Christian, had been dealing with a neurotic spinster who had used the church, the confessional, and the prayers for her own miserable purposes which ended in murder. The detective wrote to his wife, "If you believe in the God Christ preached, you must be overwhelmed by your faith, and in your time of trouble, turn with a heart of grace to prayer." Overwhelmed by your faith? Yes, if you believe in the God Christ preached.

That is where the resurrection enters in. It affirms, proclaims, and proves our faith. Paul wrote to the Romans that "Jesus Christ was declared to be the Son of God with power by the resurrection." The resurrection isn't just one man coming alive again or that you and I may, or certainly will, come alive again too. It is that God is alive. It is that God is a God of love and grace and power.

Jesus, the Jesus we love, is alive. He is risen indeed.

WHY WEEDS?

My wife suddenly looked up and propounded a question: "Why is it so much easier to be bad than good?" That has troubled people ever since there have been people. I thought of the question one day when I was digging out dandelions. In exasperation I asked it too, but in a slightly different form. "Why," I exclaimed, "do weeds flourish with such abandon and flowers have to be tended with such care or they die?"

What both of us were really asking is why God made people like they are, flowers like they are, and especially weeds like they are. Wouldn't it have been just as easy, and in fact so much better, for God and for all of us, if he had made people naturally good and flowers huskier and healthier than weeds—if he had to make weeds at all?

I can think of three answers. The first is that God *did* make us that way—and flowers too. That is one message of the Garden of Eden. There everything was natural. There were no weeds and there was no sin; or you could say just as truly that everything was weeds and everything was sin, though the truth lies in between, that there was no morality and no immorality, no flowers and no weeds as such. Life was amoral, without moral demands or implications, and nature ran rampant, with every plant both as valuable and as useless as every other.

The Garden of Eden was like a baby who is neither good nor bad, just a baby. If one wanted to return to what has been called the golden age, one would have to put up with eternal infancy. But man was not content with infancy. He developed ideals and began to reach out, believing he was intended for something higher and better than living like a cabbage, knowing neither good nor evil. But with those first yearnings toward the higher and the better there came also temptations to the opposite.

You see, goodness doesn't exist except in contrast to badness. Morality implies immorality. When man sought to rise, he had to face the danger of falling, and when God made man capable of reaching the heights, he had also to make him able to plumb the depths.

Because falling is always easier than climbing, since it requires no effort and no determination, goodness is more difficult than badness. So men take plants and cultivate them. A brier rose can with effort be developed into an American Beauty. But the very process of cultivation makes for delicacy, and the more beautiful and more highly cultivated a flower is, the less hardy it also becomes.

The second answer is that only the difficult is worth achieving. If it were as easy to be good as bad there would be little virtue in goodness. The only games worth playing or winning are those which demand skill, or strength, or patience, or all three. Honor is bestowed only on those who deserve it, and medals are given only to the brave. If we have known medals unjustly awarded and honors given which were not deserved, in every case we ourselves have scorned both the recipient and the giver. Manhood which comes naturally and without effort is of little worth, but manhood won over difficulty and danger, which overcomes handicaps and endures suffering, labor and despair, is manhood worth having.

The third answer is simply that in nature and in man there is a constant reluctance to face difficulties and hardships in order to achieve ideals and reach the heights. Plants, flowers, and people all tend to revert, to become dropouts from the school of life.

Man rebels against his burdens and tasks, and that word *rebel* is the key to it all. Weeds grow wild, but flowers have to be cultivated. Man, like the weeds, prefers his own untrammeled way, likes to be his own master and to obey no other authority. It is harder to be good than to be bad because being good is being under the authority of God and obeying his laws. It is just that simple.

FACT OR TRUTH?

Once when I mentioned the Garden of Eden a listener said to me in astonishment, "You don't believe in that, surely!"

If I had suggested the opposite opinion there probably would have been many more just as astonished and even more upset. Their exclamation would have been in the same words but with a different emphasis: "What! You *don't* believe in that?" So there I am, and there you are too, caught between two fires. We are considered foolish and credulous if we do believe, skeptical and irreligious if we don't. For me the chief difficulty is that both sides are missing the point.

The Garden of Eden, indeed the whole of the Old and New Testaments, isn't so much a fact to be accepted as a truth to be discovered.

Perhaps the best illustration is the prophecy of Jonah. That can be taken literally or figuratively, considered as an authentic history or as an allegory. Those who take it as authentic history are concerned with the big fish which swallowed Jonah, kept him in the dark and acid prison of its stomach for three days, and then spewed him out. Those who don't accept the historicity of it tend to throw the whole story over because of that same fish and its activities. But, tragically, neither group seems to have read and considered the fourth chapter. For Jonah is not primarily about a fish at all. It's about the mercy of God toward a heathen nation, the traditional enemy of him and his people, to whom Jonah and the Jews were commissioned to declare the reality, judgment, and mercy of God.

Well, to get back to Eden; is it fact or allegory? I'm not competent to say. But since I believe the Bible to be the Word of God, my concern is to try and find what God is saying in and through that story to us. What it is, is surely most clear. God is saying that he made us for himself, able to reach the heights, to be his friends, his children with whom he can have fellowship, who can love and be loved. But man wasn't satisfied to be a child—he wanted to be an equal. He refused to be merely a creation; he wanted to be a creator. "Ye shall be as gods," the serpent said.

So man turned from the proffered fellowship to have fellowship with the dark, terrible, but apparently attractive opposites. You'll find it all in the first chapter of Romans: "Because that, when they knew God, they glorified him not as God, neither were thankful; but became vain in their imaginations . . . and professing themselves to be wise they became fools, and changed the glory of the uncorruptible God into an image made like to corruptible man."

That is as true today as in the time of Paul, or the time of Jonah, or the time of those who first told the story of the Garden of Eden, ages and ages before writing was developed. The Garden of Eden is the account of the beginning of sin—pride, temptation, rebellion—and of all the misery which has come from it. You can put the Garden of Eden in the East long, long ago, in Tarsus with Paul, or in Toronto, New York, or New Orleans today.

Spiritually it is true; that is the point. Take it as you like, history or allegory, neither by itself will do you any particular good. But when you and I take it as truth, as something God is trying to say to us personally, emphatically, and today, then it really will speak to us. Surely that is what "the Word of God" means.

The story cries out that we have all sinned and come short of the glory of God. It points to our pride, selfishness, ambition, weakness, in short our sins. It shouts at us that in our hearts we still think evil attractive and goodness weak and unrewarding. Most of all it cries out to us with the tears of God himself that when he wants us as children to love and be loved, we refuse and turn away. With all that follows through the Bible it pleads with us to return to God, who forgives, and who would have us again as children beloved.

SINK OR SWIM

One of C. S. Lewis' letters reminded me that my father couldn't swim. I can still picture him striking out valiantly in fairly shallow water and getting nowhere. For twenty years or more he tried and tried to swim, but he never made it.

C. S. Lewis was writing about belief. That wasn't my father's trouble. He believed all right. He believed in swimming, he knew it could be done, and he determined that his children would do it. He insisted that a good part of the time while we were bathing each day we'd spend in learning to swim. Yes, Father believed in swimming, but he could never learn how himself. And all that gave me a mental picture of the difference between belief and faith. Father believed, but he lacked faith so far as his swimming was concerned.

For me, learning to swim was a sudden acquisition. One moment I couldn't and the next I could. Of course, for a long time I'd made splashing progress along the shore—ten, twenty, even fifty feet. But it was always a struggle, and I knew all the time that after a few more strokes I'd sink. And I did. I did until that moment when I *knew* that I could swim and keep on swimming. That was faith. It was belief put into action.

It was more than that, however. In swimming it was for me a sudden illumination. The mental block which had said insistently, "You're going to sink!" disappeared, and my mind exulted in the triumphant thought, "I'm not going to sink. I never need to sink. I can swim." That sudden illumination was as the sun bursting through the darkness of thunderclouds.

It came when I had either to swim or stay out of the water entirely. We'd moved to a cottage where the water went down ten feet deep right off the dock. There was no more beach to play on. I had either to swim or to stay out. Because I had to, I did. I put my belief into action.

That has been the way with a good deal of my religious experience too. There are some things— which I've believed in theoretically like father believed in swimming. There are other things I've tried to put into action in some kind of way, like my first puffing along in the shallow water and calling it swimming. And, thank God, there are some things where I've found faith. With every one of those things there were those three steps that I used in swimming—a theoretical belief, an attempt to put belief into action, and finally a sudden illumination and discovery. But the final step never came until I had either to have faith or to quit.

The same thing is true of the Bible, too. For instance, there is the statement of Jesus: "Seek ye first the kingdom of God, and his righteousness; and all these things shall be added unto you." You remember the context in Matthew 6. Jesus said the disciples were to take no thought of what they were to eat, drink, or wear. Jesus said that when we really sought God's kingdom those things would take care of themselves.

Theoretically I suppose we all believe that, just as many people say they believe the Bible from cover to cover—which really doesn't mean very much. I believed the statement of Jesus, theoretically. From time to time, too, I struggled with it, like puffing along in shallow water and being glad when I could put my feet on the bottom again. Then suddenly I faced what was to me a *demand* of God to go out not knowing whither I went, like Abraham. I fought against it, tried to squirm out of it, and then finally had either to obey or quit—yes, quit the ministry. So I obeyed in fear and trembling. There wasn't any shallow water, so I had either to swim or drown, figuratively speaking. When I actually launched out into the deep, I found Jesus was right. It was no longer belief but faith. I knew.

Do you see the difference? God is calling us not just to belief but to faith, to launch out into the deep, to prove him. When in fear and trembling we do that, then the sun bursts through the darkness, and the light of God shines down upon us.

WHAT HAS HE DONE FOR ME LATELY?

A man came to a friend and asked for a loan of a thousand dollars. When the friend turned him down, the man reminded him, "Harry, remember when your wife was so ill fifteen years ago, I gave her a blood transfusion? And ten years ago when your son ran away I dropped everything to go to New York to bring him back? And five years ago I loaned you three thousand dollars and saved your business?"

"Yes, yes," the friend replied, "but what have you done for me lately?"

At an air station where I was once, some very earnest young men wanted to put a box of religious tracts in the recreation hall. Now, there are tracts— and tracts. These were about as lurid as you can imagine. The C. O. turned down the request, and I tried to explain to them why. I said that on that station the airmen were faced with danger and death constantly. Then I asked, "By the way, what has God done for you this past week?"

One boy thought for a moment and said, "Well, he saved me."

"This past week?" I asked.

"Well, he kept on saving me."

I don't doubt that, nor do I want to minimize it, but I had just talked to an airman whose plane had gone into a spin, and he couldn't bring it out. Suddenly it lifted and straightened. When he landed at 3 A.M. he woke his buddy and said, "Bill, you know I haven't thought much about God. But Bill, when that plane came out, do you think God did it?"

So to me the vital question for us all is, "What has God done for me lately?" To answer "He saved me," or "He kept on saving me," isn't enough. Unless something more has happened we may well doubt the reality of that salvation.

In Bunyan's *Pilgrim Progress* Christian came to the Cross and Sepulchre, where his burden rolled away, at the beginning of his pilgrimage. Then the book goes on to describe his long and difficult road, past Giant Despair, Doubting Castle, past the lions in the way, through the city of Vanity Fair, and finally to that dark stream, the last barrier to the City of God. All the way Christian found God near at hand. God was doing something for him day by day, mile by mile.

If that has not been our experience too, we should doubt if he really did anything for us at the first, or rather if we actually took what he was trying to do. Perhaps it isn't quite fair to take *Pilgrim's Progress* as an example, for it is an allegory and difficult for any but children to understand. What we need is plain talk and personal, present-day experiences.

However, we may not be conscious of any great need to have anything done. We aren't critically ill, or weighted down with great sins which need forgiveness, or burdened with earthshaking problems to be solved. But is God only for the crises of life?

What about calmness and serenity in the face of a world gone haywire? What about a temperament which takes the stress and strain of life and is not overcome by it? What about a forgiving nature which understands when other people go off the rails and seeks to help them? What about a cheerful disposition which brings sunshine with it wherever it goes?

These may seem trivial, but they are part of the road of life and, what is more, of the nature and character of Christ. It is the process of growing into Christ and daily becoming more like him which is our real business, the assurance to ourselves and proof to others that we really have been saved.

Christianity should be living with Christ, a gay and gallant adventure, when every day gives evidence of his presence and is filled with what he has done for us, not only lately, but right now.

"ALL TOGETHER NOW, LET'S PRAY"

In *We Took to the Woods* Louise Dickinson Rich wrote about the bush telephone which connected her house with a summer hotel, a fishing lodge, the keeper of the dam, and some lumber camps. It was a battery-powered system, which meant that to call someone you turned a handle to make the correct number of rings on the other phone. Sometimes when the batteries ran down there wasn't enough power to make more than a faint tinkle, if the place you were calling was at a distance. In such circumstances you called two or three people nearer at hand and said, "Will you help me call Cliff Wiggins?" Then all the handles were turned in unison, and the combined power of the batteries was sufficient to complete the call.

And that is a hint about prayer.

Another hint came when a teacher had one pupil leave the room and the others concentrate as closely as possible on some particular thing, say a letter on the blackboard. When they did concentrate fully, the first pupil would walk at once to the thing they had chosen.

Both those hints are from practical, everyday life and show how the combined efforts of a group can do something which one person cannot do alone.

While in neither did God enter in, they do say something about prayer.

In the first place, mental power can be communicated. Some people have a capacity to impress their thoughts, wishes, even commands on others by mental telepathy. They can communicate confidence, strength, and even healing. Not the least valuable part of a doctor's equipment is a bedside manner.

In the second place, that power is multiplied enormously when a number of people use it together, but it requires effort, concentration, and intense desire. This can be entirely on a human basis without God entering in. While that isn't prayer, it does prepare our minds to think about it.

Prayer is bringing God in. It means that our human desire, effort, and concentration must be in line with God's. Suppose one of the people Mrs. Rich asked to help her had very powerful batteries, and instead of ringing one long and two short, he rang three long and one short. The result would have been chaos. If strength, healing, and hope are to be communicated through prayer the first requirement is that God's desire must be discovered, or, as we say, we must find the will of God. As Mrs. Rich first rang her neighbors to help her call Cliff Wiggins, so we must first get in touch with God.

Apparently in his wisdom there are many times when God decides to work with people. In bush telephone language, he has asked us to help him ring. He decides to use our human desires and concentration to help him do what he wants done.

The second requirement is to realize the tremendous power God has, like that of a great transmitting station to which a battery powered radio tunes in. The power of both is important; the transmitter will broadcast in vain if there are no receivers, or if the receivers are not tuned in. The power and the tuning in are equally important.

Unlike a radio, human beings can exercise their power without reference to God. It is tragic when they do, for the result can be against God's wishes and even his purposes. Most tragic of all is it when it is called prayer.

Prayer is first tuning in on God to discover his desires, then cooperating with his power, not *using* him but being used *by* him. Then human beings become workers together with God to bring hope, strength, and healing to the distressed of the world.

NOWHERE ELSE TO GO?

In a delightful book, *Grandma Called It Carnal*, Bertha Damon told of a man in prayer meeting who always began his prayer, "We come to thee, O Lord, because we have nowhere else to go." "I used to try to shut from my mind," she wrote, "the implication that if we had we'd all go there."

That reminded me of the account of the sinking

84

of the "Mariposa Belle" in Stephen Leacock's *Sun-shine Sketches of a Little Town*. The lake was shallow and there was no special danger, but the women, children, and ministers were all bundled into the leaky lifeboats. The student minister of the Presbyterian church, according to Leacock, was crouched in the bow of one boat, crying out that they were all in the hands of Providence, but ready to leap out at the earliest possible moment.

There also was the man whom Kipling seemed to admire who thought he had a pretty good chance with God because he had never bothered him unduly.

All of which seems to imply that God is not simply "our refuge and strength," as the psalmist wrote, but our *last* refuge, the one to whom we turn, as the man prayed, when there is no one else to whom we can go. In fact, isn't that what the majority of people seem to do? And isn't that the real truth behind the World War II saying that "there are no atheists in a foxhole"? Since this is too often the common conception, it is not at all surprising that, in these days of luxury, ease, and full employment, religion seems to be in a bit of a decline.

Not for a moment would I criticize anyone who comes to God in times of desperation, nor imply that God is *not* a refuge and strength, "a very present help in trouble." However, it seems to me that God should be very much more than that. A help in trouble? Yes, but even more a present and delightful companion when everything is going well.

At a young people's meeting in another city a young lady, rather lugubrious of countenance, announced that if Jesus spent all night in prayer we ought to do it too. I was rather taken aback, especially as her idea of prayer was that it should be constantly petitioning God for all kinds of things and people. "Besieging the throne of grace," it's called. Privately I thought that not only would we ourselves be literally bone weary at such a procedure, but God even more so—provided he stayed around all night to listen.

Certainly Jesus spent whole nights in prayer. So did Moses and when he came down from the mount he "wist not" that his face shone. Surely with Jesus, Moses, and the great saints of all ages, the business of prayer wasn't an extremity, when they came to God as a last resort, but a fellowship. It was a time when they could go off alone and be with God. For Jesus it was his chance to be alone with his Father, and because God was his Father in a unique and special way we cannot hope to have exactly the same experience.

But we can have one like it. In Matthew 14 the disciples returned from their preaching tour. Jesus wanted to take them off alone with him to a deserted place, but the crowds came flocking along too. The disciples were disappointed: they wanted to be alone with Jesus, to talk with him, walk with him, enjoy his company and have a good time without all those people around.

Maybe they didn't realize it (maybe we don't either) but they were praying, and they wanted more time for it.

Prayer is the presence, the fellowship, the friendship, and the gracious smile of God. It is being with someone we want to be with more than anything else, because we love him.

When we discover this, then prayer won't be the last thing we want to do, or God the last person to whom we turn, but the first.

"WELL, GOD BLESS YOU!"

I was on a bus going over a new highway in Northern Ontario. It was a lonely and lovely drive, even in winter with the snow piled high on each side. For mile after mile there was no sign of habitation, and the hamlets, when they did appear, were small and weatherbeaten. As we rounded a curve a plumpish man, dressed for the woods, waved the bus down. The driver pulled up, opened the door, and the man put a foot on the step. He smiled and asked confidentially, "Going to Winnipeg, Greyhound bus?" The driver nodded, though it wasn't a Greyhound. Then the man took his foot off the step, smiled again, and said cheerily, "Well, God bless you!" and stood aside.

87

As we went on, the driver and I smiled at each other. It was a most unconventional meeting, but a delightful one, even if it did cost us another four minutes when we were already two hours late.

What had prompted the man to come out of nowhere and stop the bus just to wish us Godspeed? Perhaps it was sheer loneliness. He probably lived in a shanty a mile or so off the road, and the bus was his only touch with people, shops, homes, and churches too—though I had a strong suspicion he was not unfamiliar with spirits of another kind. Maybe it would take something like that to give him enough courage to stop the bus and say, "Well, God bless you" to driver and passengers.

That incident made me think of other lonely people—you perhaps. Did you ever think of stopping a bus? It might be a good idea at that. If you don't dare go that far, however, maybe there is something else you'd like to do, if you had the courage. Loneliness is often lack of courage. It isn't lack of people; it is lack of companionship. More people are lonely in a big city than in the wilderness. But in city or wilderness there are people somewhere, even if it is just on a bus speeding at sixty miles an hour down the highway. No, the problem isn't lack of people—it is getting in touch with them.

Then why don't we do it? The man in the forest did, and I hope he felt better for it—we certainly did. However, you don't have to flag down a bus; there are other simpler and more conventional ways. It does require courage to stop anyone, even if he isn't a bus. I know. I was born shy—a horrible and unnecessary condition. I've recovered, I'm glad to say, and I've found it is exciting and rewarding to stop people and talk to them.

I did it in Edinburgh. There were some large buildings I was curious about, so I stopped a man and asked him about them. He told me what he knew, and we chatted for a while, partly about Canada, where he had been during the war. Then he insisted on taking me down the street to see one of the few waterwheels in the world still at work. We parted as friends, each brightened by the meeting.

I stopped a policeman in London (surely the height of temerity) to ask if the two pips on his shoulder meant that he was an inspector. They did, and for a few moments we talked of detective stories.

I chat with all kinds of people—waitresses, nurses, bus drivers (not all the time, of course). This is the interesting thing about it: they are all glad to be spoken to. They smile and talk back and seem happier at the end. For you see, they are lonely too.

And *you* are lonely. Well, you aren't the only one. In addition to the lack of courage which afflicts us, another problem is that we think too much about our own loneliness and not enough about the loneliness of others. I know people appear so self-sufficient, so aloof, and seem to have their guards up. Certainly! That's a sign of loneliness—the way we look ourselves. But how quickly the guard comes down when a friend appears. And you can be that friend.

You are still apprehensive about what reception you'll get? There is one thing which opens the hearts and unseals the lips of almost everyone— the chance to be of assistance. People are really glad to answer questions, give necessary information, and put you on the right road. Approach them for assistance, and the doors will open.

The doors will open, especially if you have in your heart the wish for them that the man in the forest had on his lips, "Well, God bless you!" If that is what you want for them and for yourself, you'll never need to be lonely. For not the least of God's blessings is friendship for the lonely.

PUTTING GOD TO WORK

I never felt the problem of unemployment so keenly as during the depression. It was bad enough to see hundreds of men in the parks playing cards, talking, or just sitting around despondently, but it was far worse to meet other men who were feverishly and desperately looking for work—any kind of work—and finding none at all.

Yet there was lots of work which needed to be done. Houses went unpainted, buildings, unrepaired, sidewalks unmended. The very parks where the unemployed sat in idleness were littered with waste paper and refuse. Yes, there was work, lots of it, necessary work, but no one did it. The problem wasn't lack of work but lack of money to pay for it.

While it is always distressing to see men and women with nothing to do, it is much more distressing to see God with nothing to do. An idle God? It sounds fantastic, but it's true.

Jesus spoke about the unemployed in the marketplace who, when asked why they sat idle, said it was because no man had hired them. That is the secret of unemployment in all ages. That is also the secret of God's unemployment—no man has hired him.

You see, God is not self-employed. He doesn't set out to do things by himself regardless of people. In his wisdom he has limited himself and chosen to work for men only at their definite request, if they hire him so to speak. They have to see what needs doing and ask God to do it.

A decorator, say, needs work. He points out that the walls in our living room are dingy, ugly, and cracked, and that the paint is peeling off in the kitchen. He'd like to get the job of redecorating. He brings testimonials as to the quality of his workmanship. Whether he gets the job or not depends on us; we have to hire him to do it.

So too God has pointed out repeatedly and unmistakably the work which needs to be done. He has shown clearly that he is abundantly able to do it, pointing out similar work done for others. He's even furnished testimonials. Beyond that, apparently, God cannot or will not go. We have to hire him to do the work.

What work? Well, for instance there are the past sins which plague and stain us, like the splotched walls in our living rooms, made ugly by the crude drawings scrawled on them in our childhood. Those reminders of past follies horrify us and reveal to other people the darkness of our past. So we cover them up as best we can by putting pictures over them and rearranging the furniture. But it doesn't work very well, does it? We're always afraid someone will move something and see them.

God can clean that up, and only God can do it. He is willing to come in and change all the ugliness, making it clean, wholesome, and beautiful. All the preparations have been made and he is anxious to get at it. The forgiveness has already been given through the cross of Christ. All that remains is for us to call him and let him work. But until we do that, nothing can happen.

There are our present sins, weaknesses, and temptations too, which so often overcome us. Perhaps most of all there is our lack of development, so that our dreams of the kind of person we meant to be, could be, have never been realized. We haven't been able to do much about those things ourselves, have we? God says *he* can. He brings testimonials from Peter, Paul, Augustine, Wesley, Bunyan, and thousands of others. Then God has to wait. He can't do anything till we hire him.

There are the problems and perplexities of life too—sickness, sorrow, bewilderment. We see no path ahead, no way out. Then God comes and says that if we hire him he will be our guide. Can he? Listen to the testimony of the psalmist, "Yea, though I walk through the valley of the shadow of death, I will fear no evil: for thou art with me." Yes, he can guide, if we hire him.

Hire? What do we mean by hire? What does God charge, and have we money enough to pay it?

All God asks is that we own him as God, trust him, believe in him, give our lives into his keeping, take his love, and love him in return.

Is that too much to pay?

WITNESSES

Any reader of Perry Mason has undoubtedly developed a profound sympathy for people subpoenaed to be witnesses at a trial. Poor witnesses! They testify to the best of their ability, and then the lawyer gets hold of them. "Are you sure, Mr. X, that it was a woman you saw?" "Yes, a woman with a black coat, brown hair, and blue eyes." "And you were a hundred feet away?" "Yes." "And from that distance you can swear that it was a woman with a brown coat and black hair?" "No, I said a black coat, brown hair, and blue eyes." And so it goes, back and forth, until the witness doesn't know what color his own hair is, whether it was a woman or not, or whether she had on any coat at all.

No wonder the Greek word for witness was *martus,* a martyr. That seems to be what a witness becomes. It is no wonder either that most of us are determined never to be witnesses if any power on earth can get us out of it. We have an aversion to being martyrs. So we keep discreetly aloof, and the cause of justice suffers because we don't want to be involved.

It isn't only the cause of justice which suffers from reluctant witnesses. Christianity suffers too. Jesus, at his ascension, told the disciples that they were to be witnesses unto him—and look what happened to them! Martyrs is right! No wonder most Christians not only hesitate to be, but in most cases carefully avoid being, witnesses. They don't want to be martyrs too, thank you.

However, whether we like it or not, witnessing is one thing we can't help doing. Maybe we think that by keeping our mouths shut we avoid it, but we don't. We may not be witnesses unto Christ, but all the time, everywhere, and to everyone we meet we are witnessing to something, to the kind of religion we have—or to our lack of it.

Take the very fact that we try to avoid becoming involved and to leave all witnessing to ministers who are paid to do it. That in itself is a witness to our cowardice (though we may prefer to call it prudence), or it shouts aloud that Jesus means so little to us that we refuse to get into any hot water on his account.

Witnessing has two meanings: first, seeing, and second, testifying about what was seen. In his first letter John wrote, "That which we have seen and heard declare we unto you." He used both meanings of the word. A witness has seen something, and in a court of law that must be firsthand, not hearsay evidence. No witness is allowed to testify to what someone else has told him.

Maybe that is one of our troubles in Christianity. So many of us have seen nothing firsthand. What we have has too often come through tradition or sermons, out of books, or from the creed. We ourselves can't vouch for it, we just heard it. We believe it might be true, but you can't rely on us for proof. Yes, I think that is one difficulty with much of our Christian witnessing; it is secondhand. When we are not personally sure, we don't dare tell others.

But we don't need to. Whether Christian experience is firsthand or secondhand is easy to discover just by looking at or living with people for a time. And, thank God, we all know many who by their lives give witness to the power of God in Jesus Christ.

Yes, if our witness is firsthand, if Christ has really reached down into our hearts, touched our lives, met us on our Damascus Road, it will stick out all over. Some churches ask for evidences of regeneration before admitting one to membership. That simply means that a person should show some results of having met Christ. It won't be shown in words first, but in conduct, in a certain, though immature, Christlikeness of character.

And if all this has happened, in almost every case the witness begins to witness too. For one result of Christ's hand upon us is that we count it an honor to be a martyr for him, a witness of him who has loved, touched, and redeemed us.

FATAL LITERALISM

If you plan on making a will, go to a lawyer. The small amount he'll charge may save an awful lot of trouble and perhaps mean that the persons to whom you plan to leave your estate will really get it. Otherwise they may not.

When you draw up your own will, you fully intend to let cousin Doris have a thousand dollars, Aunt Sadie five hundred, and your niece Henrietta all the rest. To you your intention may be as clear as crystal, but the law has no regard for your intentions. The law cannot read your mind, sometimes it is hard enough to read your writing. So the law has to go by the words you write, and only a lawyer knows the exact words to express what you intend so it will be fully carried out. In a will there are two things, the intention and the wording—or, putting it in biblical language, the letter and the spirit. And in a will too often "the letter killeth" the intention because the intention could not be fully understood.

Paul also talked of these three—wills, wording, and intention. In II Corinthians 3:6 he wrote, "Who also hath made us able ministers of the new testament [the last will and testament of Jesus Christ]; not of the letter, but of the spirit [the wording and the intention]: for the letter killeth, but the spirit giveth life" [the possible tragedy—and the way out].

The tragedy has been not just possible but all too prevalent. It happened in Paul's day when the Judaizers nearly wrecked Christianity by insisting that all converts be subject to the whole Jewish law. It happened in Jesus' day when the Pharisees, as he said, tithed mint and cummin, neglecting the really vital matters, emphasized the Sabbath and neglected mercy and humanity. And it happens today, as often, I'm afraid, as ever in history.

Paul was afraid of that too. He warned the Corinthians, his fellow ministers, and all Christians of the peril. They were all in danger of so emphasizing some of the wording that they would kill the very intention of Christ. Paul nowhere said it better than in I Corinthians 13: "Though I speak with the tongues of men and of angels, and have not love, I am become as sounding brass or a tinkling

97

cymbal; and though I have the gift of prophecy, and understand all mysteries and all knowledge, and though I have all faith so that I could remove mountains, and have not love, I am nothing."

Paul knew what he was talking about. After all, he had done that once himself, keeping the law scrupulously, versed in the Old Testament as were few others. He was exceedingly zealous for his God, and a hard, mean, murderous devil of a man he was too! "The letter killeth, but the spirit giveth life." Yes, Paul found that out to his cost and the sorrow of many Christian converts.

Now, regarding the New Testament of Jesus Christ, which means his will and the will of God—what is its spirit? What was its intention? That should be easy to discover. Surely God didn't veil it in verbiage, hide it in mysterious passages hard to be understood by any save the initiated, or put it in cryptic words and phrases capable of several interpretations. Surely it is clear, emphatic, and certain. So let us let the rest go, for the time at least, and find out what Jesus said most often, most emphatically, and most clearly. That will be his will and testament, telling us where he wanted his estate to go.

This may sound too simple, but a will should be simple. It may sound too inclusive, perhaps letting in many whom we'd rather see kept out, but that is Jesus' business, not ours. But this is the clear, unmistakable intention of Jesus, his last will and testament. Yes, it will be as clear, as sure and as simple as his words, "Come unto me all ye that labour and are heavy laden, and I will give you rest."

WHEN YOUR WORLD ENDS

Every spring we go up to the cottage for a few hours to see how it has come through the winter. One year the trees were all standing, the dock had come through with flying colors, but the roof had leaked. It had leaked in two places, one right over our bed.

My wife said "Tut! tut!" (or words to that effect) and opened the window so the bed could dry off a little. Down onto the bed dropped three completely naked babies. They were flying squirrels, and their nest of shredded cedar hung precariously over the window ledge. Mama flying squirrel had found a small hole in the shutter just large enough to squeeze through and had built her nest and had her babies in that apparently safe niche. Then her world suddenly came to an end. The window opened, her babies were spilled on the floor, and she was panic-stricken.

My wife called me to take the shutter off, while she gathered up the babies and nest on a tray. Mama squirrel leaped out of the window and ran up a birch tree in a fever of chattering anxiety. We opened the toolshed, put nest and babies on the second shelf, and left the door open. When I looked again, the nest had been moved to the first shelf so I propped the door partly open, wired it so it couldn't open farther, and left them in their new home. That adventure tickled us, and we were quite pleased with ourselves that we were kind enough to try and patch up a disaster that was really no one's fault.

Later I began to wonder about God. Is he as generous, thoughtful, and interested in people as we were with the squirrels?

Even to hint at that question may seem like a slap in the face of God. It would be much simpler to say that God is far more thoughtful, sympathetic, considerate, and helpful than people can ever be. But really the problem isn't nearly that simple.

In Matthew 10:28-31 Jesus told the disciples that God would take care of them in the face of the trials he foretold. But it was rather strange encouragement. "Fear not them which kill the body," he said, "but are not able to kill the soul: but rather fear him which is able to destroy both soul and body in hell. Are not two sparrows sold for a farthing? and one of them shall not fall on the ground without your Father. . . . Fear ye not therefore, ye are of more value than many sparrows."

Yes, but sparrows did fall to the ground; the apostles, all but John, were martyred; and Jesus himself was crucified. Jesus said, "Fear not them which kill the body," and bodies are killed, and sparrows constantly fall to the ground. We teach children the hymn "This is my Father's world," but we forget to mention the shriek of a rabbit caught in the claws of a hawk or the gleeful chattering of a squirrel which has just robbed a bird's nest.

It might be wiser to omit all this and say that, just as we carefully replaced the squirrel's nest, so God cares for and looks after us. But can we forget the cross of God's own Son and the martyrdom of his followers? Can we forget the sparrows which fall, or our own predicaments either?

Into the office of a minister burst a grief-stricken father, frantic with grief and filled with rage against God who had let his son be killed in a car accident. "Where was your God when my son was killed?" he stormed to the minister. The minister looked at him with understanding and pity. "In exactly the same place he was when his own Son was killed," he answered.

Is that good enough, or isn't it? That is the question we have to answer. Maybe it doesn't seem to be when our world apparently ends. We forget that our world *must* end, for it is material, spun of the gossamer web of time. If there is another world, a world of the spirit, infinite and eternal, that makes all the difference. When a sparrow falls, God is there with it, Jesus said. God falls with each sparrow.

When we have figured out that strange statement, we may find something far greater, more lasting, and more filled with love than the mere replacing of a squirrel's nest.

101

WATER BUGS AND DRAGONFLIES

Near an old log farmhouse, where we spent some summers when I was a boy, a corduroy road crossed a stream over a bridge and a dam. From the dam a timber chute led across the rocks to carry logs in the spring drive. The chute was covered with what looked like skeletons, each with six wiry legs gripping the wood with the intensity of death, a lifeless head, and a round shell of a body split up the back. They were the shells of the water insects from which dragonflies had emerged.

As a boy I'd watch the dragonflies whizzing like demented jets in the air around me and then look at the skeletons clinging to the wood of the chute just above the water line, and I'd wonder about them. I'm still wondering.

What prompted the insect to begin the climb out of the water? All its life had been spent in the water, above which the faint blue of the surface bounded its horizon as surely as the sky does ours. It swam around in the only world it knew, until suddenly an urge seized it. It started to climb, broke the surface, and disappeared. I suppose to all the other insects, as to my boyish mind, the bodies clinging to the timbers were corpses, skeletons.

I'd turn from the brittle shells on the timbers to

watch the dragonflies circling overhead, darting, soaring, swerving, diving. The air was their delight, their playground, as if they had been released from dark imprisonment. Having been waterbound they suddenly discovered a new and far more wonderful element. Having faced death in dread they found instead the most exciting, glorious life which could be imagined.

How could one tell that to the insects still within their little pools, the only world there was to them? How could one tell them of the boundless sky, the sunshine, the beauty of the flowers and trees, the sparkle of sunlight on the surface of the water, and above all, the splendor of flight? How could one tell them that instead of a dumpy body they would be long and slight with gossamer wings not only to make them beautiful, but to lift them high into the air and send them swirling and dancing in the magic of flight?

One couldn't, of course. No dragonfly had ever come back, or could ever come back, how could they recognize it as one of themselves if it did? No, all they had was that urge, that instinct for apparent death, to send them so reluctantly, yet so remorselessly, up beyond the water line. Then followed the agony of a bursting body so evident in the feet gripping the wood so tenaciously that weeks later they had to be pried off by force.

Here were two elements—two worlds—the lower so different that none within it could conceive what the other could possibly be like. Here was the slow movement of an ugly water insect and the dazzling speed of a creature of gorgeous beauty. Yet both were the same insect.

We too are creatures of one world and are utterly incapable of comprehending any other. Speak to us of a world of the spirit, and we stare without comprehension. Tell us that those whose bodies we have buried have been released to a world so much more wonderful than this, and we practical, material mortals cannot understand.

Yet for us there are echoes of that other world here and now. At times it comes so close we can almost see it. It is not clarion clear, it cannot and should not be, but all around, for those with eyes to see and ears to hear, are evidences that somewhere it exists, somewhere it is waiting.

From that world has come a messenger, Jesus. In himself, in his life, his words, and his actions, he showed the reality of that other world, even though on earth he was imprisoned in a body like ours. After he did what men call *die,* he returned briefly, to be seen and heard and to call men to follow him.

All who saw, heard, and followed found something of the beauty of that other world growing in themselves too. We can find it also. By following Jesus we can find in our hearts and souls a reflection of the beauty and reality of that world which awaits us after what men call *death.*

PROVING THE LIFE BEYOND

One day a friend asked me a challenging question: "Can you prove there is life beyond the grave?"

It wasn't argumentative, frivolous, or idle. He was just recovering from his second stroke. I couldn't give an idle answer, or a stock-in-trade one, traditional, accepted, usual. In all frankness and honesty I had to say, "No, I can't."

Of course I went on to say why I myself believed there was, though I had to admit my belief was, in a large measure, hope that there was. But when the chips were down, I had to admit honestly that if it was *proof* which was demanded, I couldn't give it. Nor could any man.

Later I remembered some advice given by a famous preacher to his students: "Preach as a dying man to dying men." When my friend asked his question, he was in a sense a dying man—a consciously dying man. For the first time he was facing the fact that it was he himself, not somebody else, who was going to die. Before me was a dying man, and I had no proof. Hope, yes; faith, yes; but proof, no.

Then one day both my friend's question and the preacher's advice came back to me. I was myself in the shoes of my friend. I was facing the fact of my mortality. Like my friend I found it a devastating experience.

Of course I had accepted it theoretically long before. Indeed when I had stood on the deck of a troopship waiting to put out into the submarine-infested Atlantic I thought I had faced it practically too. But even then it was only theory. This time, though, it was direct, personal, and all too possibly immediate.

As I thought of the preacher's advice, "Preach as a dying man to dying men," it seemed to me there was something artificial about it. How can one preach as a dying man except he be in reality, not just in theory, a dying man? And how can one preach to dying men except they are also in reality dying men? And when you get both together, you'll find something far different from what you might imagine.

Preach as a dying man? Well, how? I'll tell you how—with a blankness and grayness than which there is nothing so blank or gray. I didn't think it would be that way. I was horrified at myself. Then I remembered the supreme case of a dying man preaching to dying men. In John 13-17 there are tremendous words of comfort, faith, and hope, spoken by Jesus the night before he died. Perhaps we think those were the words of a dying man to dying men, but they weren't. It was the next day he died. And it was then that we hear that terrible cry from the cross, "My God, my God, why hast thou forsaken me?"

There it is, like it or not. There is blankness, grayness, desolation. I'm glad our Saviour went through it too; it doesn't make me feel so bad that it was gray for me also. There was no glib assurance then, no easy acceptance; not for my friend, or for me—or for Jesus. There was only faith, love, and hope. There is no other proof except in those three for any of us. But perhaps there is ground enough in them.

If the Bible closed with the cross it would end in failure. Even if it closed with the last chapters of the Gospels, it would end with what so many skeptics have called the wishful thinking of the discomfited disciples, vainly imagining that their Jesus was somehow still alive. But the Bible *doesn't* end there; in fact, it hasn't ended yet. It goes on to Pentecost, to the early church, to the apostle Paul and to all that has happened since. It goes on to an admittedly imperfect Church (after all, it is composed of people like you and me), but a church which has had its tremendous heroes, its great moments, its sacrificial lives, its heroic deaths, its abiding faith, hope, and love, and its continuing life.

That isn't proof. As Paul said, we walk by faith and not by sight. And like my friend who asked the question we all have an inner yearning and hope, an instinct for life beyond. Like Tennyson we cry,

107

Strong Son of God, immortal Love,
>   Whom we, that have not seen thy face,
>   By faith, and faith alone, embrace,
> Believing where we cannot prove. . . .
> We have but faith: we cannot know.

But we do have faith—that inner spark, that deep-down yearning, that inmost sense of the justice and love of God. In the hour when we are indeed dying men, when there is only blankness and grayness within us, as there was for Jesus, then we'll know how futile all our discussions and arguments have been. We'll know that only two things in all the world matter at all, ourselves and God.

Blessed shall we be then if our God is like Jesus Christ.

LIGHT FROM THE DARKNESS

A young woman I know recently came to a new understanding of God. Formerly God had been for her someone to fear, sitting up somewhere with a black pencil in his hand checking off all our faults and good points, especially our faults. He did it avidly, gloating over each black mark, waiting, almost hoping, that the faults would outweigh the good points so he could punish us.

Then she discovered that God isn't like that at all. He's a God of love.

It was the way she found this out that startled me. She said it was in two events, first when her father died some years ago, and then within the last year when a favorite nephew, a boy of ten, died suddenly. It startled me because it is in just such experiences that so many people lose what faith they had, turn against God as an ogre, a cruel despot, and have nothing more to do with him. Yet my friend, in those very circumstances, said she really discovered that God is a God of love. One is tempted to ask, "How can such things be?"

Then I remembered. I went back a good many years to when I was seventeen, and my brother and I represented the family at Father's funeral. I endured the services in the house and at the church. I hardly heard the words of the eulogy, thought how vague was the solo, "Beautiful Isle of Somewhere," and then sat unthinking through the slow procession to the cemetery. Then, as I stood beside the grave, something spoke to me. It wasn't the minister, but words formed in my own mind, kind, emphatic, assuring words. "I go to prepare a place for you. And if I go and prepare a place for you, I will come again, and receive you unto myself; that where I am, there ye may be also."

Of all the experiences of my life that is one that stands out. To my mind, then and now, it seemed to me that a kind and loving God took the trouble to bring personal comfort to a boy in distress.

At that very same place twelve years later again something spoke to me. Our first boy at thirteen

109

months was being buried beside his grandfather. As I stood, within inches of where I had stood before, other words came. "Those who sleep in Jesus will the Lord bring with him when he comes." I thought of a lonely little baby taken by the hand by two grandfathers while Jesus looked on, smiling in love and compassion.

I don't know whether it fits exactly, but Samson's riddle comes to my mind: "Out of the eater came forth meat." It suggests to me that out of disaster can come comfort. There are a good many other places in the Bible where that same sunlight streams through the clouds.

"Yea, though I walk through the valley of the shadow of death, I will fear no evil: for thou art with me; thy rod and thy staff they comfort me," sang the psalmist. Isaiah spoke for God, "When thou passest through the waters, I will be with thee; and through the rivers, they shall not overflow thee." And there was the triumphant experience of Paul, on trial before the emperor; "All men forsook me: . . . Notwithstanding the Lord stood with me, and strengthened me; . . . and I was delivered out of the mouth of the lion."

So from my own experience and that of men of old I turn back to the young woman who found God's love in what seems to many such strange places, and I understand. One of her explanations may help you to understand. About the death of her nephew she said, "God permitted me to be of use."

Perhaps that is the highest privilege of all—"God

permitted me to be of use." I recall Harry Emerson Fosdick writing about a young man who came to him with grave doubts. Dr. Fosdick had other pressing duties, one of which was the problem of another young man who was so despondent he was contemplating suicide. Fosdick, having to keep another engagement, sent the doubter to the second man, and from that encounter the doubter came back, his doubts gone. God had permitted him to be of use.

It may be that *our* doubts will also vanish, and we will find faith and be sure that God is a God of love if we let ourselves be of use too.